**James Borg** is an award-winning  author whose books have been tran\: languages. His 2008 book *Persuasiu\_\. in popular psychology, as well as spending a record-breaking 118 consecutive weeks at number one in the WHSmith Travel Business chart. In 2013, *Persuasion* was one of only three publications by UK authors (along with those by Sir Richard Branson and Sir James Dyson) to be featured in *Future* magazine's '50 Best Business Books' of all time.

As a specialist in interpersonal communications, body language and the mind, Borg runs occasional workshops relating to 'mind control' and on how to develop a super memory.

He contributes regularly to newspapers, magazines and radio on topics related to his writings, as well as travel and sports, and was invited to be a contributor to *Harvard Business Review*.

## Praise for James Borg

'This book is spot-on and should be a must-read'
*Daily Telegraph*

'A rare "self-help" book. Marvellously readable and fun.
Hugely to be recommended'
Jilly Cooper, bestselling author

'A highly readable, authoritative and indispensable handbook for
all of us who need other people to do what we want'
Sir Antony Jay, writer and creator of BBC's *Yes Minister* and *Yes, Prime Minister*

'James is a smart and perceptive juggler of words.
I'm just hoping he doesn't start writing lyrics'
Don Black, Oscar-winning lyricist

'A fascinating book'
Steve Wright, BBC Radio 2, *Steve Wright in the Afternoon*

'Fascinating reading for anyone who wants to be more
effective in life, and in any social group!'
Gillian Tett, award-winning columnist and journalist at the *Financial Times*

'This is a handy, readable guide ... The author persuaded
me to review this book. Damn, he is good'
Jeremy Vine, *The Times*

'An author of inspirational works'
*Independent*

'Barack Obama was once asked which book he would take to
the White House if he became President. His reply was "Abraham
Lincoln's". Sadly, I couldn't think of any which I held in
similar esteem. However, James Borg's book starts to
address this situation'
*Supply Management* magazine

'I give full credit to James Borg. I recommend you read the book in full. It's a potential life changer'
*Life Coach Directory*

'*Mind Power* is the best of the current self-help books'
*Guardian*

'I'm persuaded that this book is an essential aid in getting people on your side. Invaluable'
Sue Lawley, BBC radio and TV presenter

'Persuaded? We were. Buy it'
*Management Today*

'It is definitely a five-star read'
*San Francisco Book Review*

'One of the bestselling self-help books of the 21st century'
Philip Stone, Charts Editor, *The Bookseller*

'Borg is an expert on body language'
*The Times*

'Leaves you with the satisfaction of knowing that, by the end of the book, you have taken your communication skills to a whole new level'
Angela Rippon, radio and TV broadcaster

'Intelligent and rational ways in which everyone can get their neurons firing and improve their thinking. Its light-hearted and enthusiastic style makes this one of the better self-help books out there'
*Booksquawk*

'A witty and fast-paced journey ... There are some real gems in this book'
*Edge* magazine

# JAMES BORG

# IS THAT YOUR CARD?

Control Your Thinking. Change Your Life.
Improve Your Mental Health.

ROBINSON

ROBINSON

First published in Great Britain in 2023
by Robinson

10 9 8 7 6 5 4 3 2 1

A CIP catalogue record for this book
is available from the British Library.

ISBN: 978-1-47214-497-3

Typeset in Sentinel and Scala Sans
by Mousemat Design Limited.

Printed and bound in Great Britain by
Clays Ltd, Elcograf S.p.A.

Papers used by Robinson are from well-
managed forests and other responsible
sources.

MIX
Paper from
responsible sources
FSC® C104740

Robinson
An imprint of
Little, Brown Book Group
Carmelite House
50 Victoria Embankment
London EC4Y 0DZ

An Hachette UK Company
www.hachette.co.uk

www.littlebrown.co.uk

*I would like to dedicate this book to HM Queen Elizabeth II. Despite her privileged upbringing, she was dealt a challenging hand at a relatively early age in which she had to face an untimely and unexpected elevation as our monarch both here in the United Kingdom and in other realms.*

*With her quiet stoicism, skillful mastery of emotions and selfless devotion to duty, for over seventy years in a rapidly changing world she captivated the hearts of people across the globe.*

*Model yourself on card players . . . externals I cannot control, but the choices I make with regard to them, I do control.*
*ENCHIRIDION* EPICTETUS (*C.* AD 125)

*Each player must accept the cards life deals him or her;
but once they are in hand, he or she alone must decide
how to play the cards in order to win the game.*
VOLTAIRE (1694–1788)

# Contents

Foreword by Dr Sian Williams     xiii

**Introduction:** You are what you think     1

**The meeting**     7

**Session 1** Is That Your Card?
It's the stories we tell ourselves     17

**Session 2** Psychological Stress and 'Stressors'
Taking care of your mental health     35

**Session 3** The Ancient Philosophy of the Stoics
What would Epictetus, Seneca and Marcus Aurelius say?     61

**Session 4** It's as Easy as ABC
From ancient philosophy to modern psychology     81

**Session 5** Worry and Anxiety
The power of irrational thinking     101

**Session 6** Tame that Anger
It's the tip of the 'iceberg'     123

**Session 7** The Gods May Throw the Dice
You've played all your cards     143

**The discussion**     157

# Foreword

**Dr Sian Williams, counselling psychologist and broadcaster**

We all face moments of doubt. Times when we feel out of control, can't cope, let negative thoughts and feelings derail us. That's when we need a guide to help us back on the path to good mental health and wellbeing.

*Is That Your Card?* recognises that we can all be dealt a bad hand – but it's how we react to it that defines us. Our recovery from adversity is affected by the stories we tell, the value judgements we make and the self-talk that can hold us back.

James draws from the ancient wisdom of the Stoic philosophers to modern cognitive psychologists to help us understand how to navigate challenging times. And he poses a question: if that IS your card, how will you choose to play it?

*Sian Williams started her broadcast career with the BBC in 1985 as a journalist, eventually moving on from her Radio 4 current affairs editing and producing work to her prolific television news anchor and presenting roles. This included the sofa of* BBC Breakfast *from 2001–2012, while she was also a key figure in BBC One's news-reading team. For two successive years, Sian won the 'News Presenter of the Year' award at the Television and Radio Industries Club (TRIC) Annual Awards.*

*She moved over to ITN in 2016 as the presenter of Channel 5's* 5 News *(until 2022) and introduced a weekly segment concerning mental health, called* Mind Matters.

*Concurrent with her broadcasting work, she had been working as a psychological therapist in the NHS and studying for a Doctorate in counselling psychology, which she was awarded in 2021. Sian has returned to BBC Radio 4 as a psychologist to present the series* Life Changing, *exploring people's stories about resilience and renewal.*

# Introduction

## You are what you think

We all have daily challenges and traumas to get through, ranging from domestic, professional and financial issues to concerns about health and interpersonal relationships. Is it any wonder that poor mental health is something that millions of people live with from day to day?

In the last decade or so we've seen a distinct shift in the understanding of 'mental health'. Previously it was a term that was associated with mental 'ill' health, but now, quite rightly, it is used to denote our mental well-being in everyday life.

Life's 'cards' – the circumstances and challenges dealt out to all of us – naturally make a big difference to our lives. Yet some people with a 'good hand' may not succeed in life as well as somebody who is dealt a 'poor hand'.

I can vividly remember as a child hearing the words, 'Is that your card?' when a magician had performed a magic effect involving a pack of playing cards. When I was a little older I 'fell' into the company of magicians.

As my interest in magic turned into a fascination, I was proud to be admitted, when just a teenager, as one of the youngest-ever members of Britain's oldest magical society. I specialised in 'mind magic', which furthered my later interest in psychology. Soon I found myself uttering those same words, 'Is that your card?', to an audience. All this in the days before Hogwarts and Harry Potter had been conceived in the fertile mind of J.K. Rowling!

Not long after, I came across this passage during my studies:

*Model yourself on card players. The chips don't matter
and the cards don't matter; how can I know what the
deal will be? But making careful and skilful use of the
deal – that's where my responsibility begins . . .
externals I cannot control, but the choices I make with
regard to them, I do control.*
ENCHIRIDION EPICTETUS (C. AD 125)

Now the concept of 'cards' took on another meaning in a philosophical sense: the cards, or hand, you were dealt in life.

This quote was from a Greek Stoic philosopher. My interest in the Stoic philosophy was kindled during my university studies a few decades ago, when economics confirmed itself as living up to its description as the 'dismal science'. I found it was psychology that was more pertinent to life (*and* economics) and this discovery shaped my eventual interests and further graduate studies.

In tandem with that, it was the study of its close cousin, philosophy – or rather one particular 'school' of it – that resonated deeply with me: the philosophy of the Stoics from more than two thousand years ago.

Unlike other earlier philosophies, it was a philosophy of a way of life, of how to live. And, more importantly, how to think. It showed how to deal with life's daily adversities and live a good life. Its attraction was that it was a *practical* way of conducting the art of living (we'll explore that later in this book).

For the Stoics the principle was simple: you are what you think. Your thoughts create your reality – for good or bad – and they influence everything you say, feel and do.

They were aware of the inner narrative that operates in the background of our minds, and which is responsible for everything we think, feel, say and do. They were all too aware that the words we use have tremendous power: they evoke an emotional state which results in a specific type of action or behaviour. More importantly, they recognised that this applies to both our inner dialogue and the words we use in everyday encounters.

These Stoic ideas resonated with my own thinking that you can gain insight, inspiration and motivation from studying wisdom passed down from long ago. Then you can take the principles with which you identify to help guide you in your own path in life.

Years later, during my postgraduate studies in psychology and psychotherapy, I came across the works of the American psychologist and psychotherapist Dr Albert Ellis. Later a business trip to New York enabled me to visit the Albert Ellis Institute over on East 32nd Street, which proved very inspiring; this pioneer of cognitive therapy was heavily influenced by the readings of the Stoics. The pieces of the 'jigsaw' were starting to come together ...

Ellis's therapy was based on the premise that we form subjective impressions and become upset and troubled by our own value judgements rather than by things themselves. According to Ellis, it is our thinking that is at the core of the 'disturbance' that we all face in life. So clearly the Stoic philosophers directly influenced the development of modern-day cognitive therapies.

This fusion of ancient philosophy with modern-day psychology has provided us with a valuable personal 'operating system' for life.

Having enjoyed a lifelong fascination with the psychology of the mind and human behaviour, I've spent much of my career (and personal study) looking at the twin areas of the power of *persuasion* in human communication as well as the huge influence of our *body language*. But there's a third strand: our *thinking*. Nothing happens without our thought process, and being aware that this is something within our control can change our life.

I've been interested in trying to fathom out the reason why some individuals, who appear to have everything that could lead to a successful and satisfying life, display and experience the opposite. Then, by comparison, there are the others who start out with so much less, yet go on to achieve good or great things, in all areas of life. Our thinking plays a huge part in these outcomes.

Some people have the self-awareness to recognise that thinking is not something that just happens to us, but is something we *do*. It's the starting point for everything and it goes a long way in minimising a life of stress, anxiety and suffering, and creating a life of greater satisfaction, success and mental resilience.

We have most of our conversations with ourselves; words and language are important not just in our writing and exchanges with other people, but in our conversations with *ourselves*. Words are powerful. They arouse strong emotional responses within us.

I've always been particularly moved by song lyrics, especially those that comfort and hold a special meaning. Words that provide you with important life lessons – and that can *change* your thinking. Those lyrics that lift your mood, get you through sad and difficult times, help you understand your own deficiencies and inspire you to pursue your dreams . . . before it's too late.

Who can resist the poetic pen of a songwriter when it's expressed by the voice of the matchless Karen Carpenter, urging us to look to our dreams, lest the future may say we can blame blind yesterday for chasing dreams away.

Even now I can't think of anything that matches the joy of good melodies and lyrics. Consequently, my first 'wish list' career choice was obvious – to be a songwriter. Not much joy with the careers officer. Then radio – a weekly BBC Radio slot. Still no joy. Then back to reality.

What was clear to me was that there is a 'magical' power that we can assign to words. We cast spells with our language. Is there something we can deduce from the fact that the word 'spell' has a dual meaning? You could say that we cast a 'spell' with words and also have to arrange letters in a specific order to 'spell' words.

There is an 'alchemy' associated with language. If we change the way we think, we're using different language which then changes our feelings and subsequent behaviour. Then 'magic happens'. So in that sense we're all linguistic alchemists. It's our 'superpower'.

As we'll discuss later, we're all storytellers in life and it's the stories we tell ourselves that determine the path we take. In addition, from childhood onwards we're predisposed to listening, remembering and telling stories. Quite often, to help illustrate a point, we'll use a story. They also help us to learn. We connect with stories emotionally. We know that stories make words come alive.

In that vein, I begin our 'journey' with a story, which I hope will help illustrate the power you have in taking some control over events in your life and at the same time improve your mental well-being.

# The meeting

Back from his six-month secondment at his company's New York headquarters, Jon settled into his seat in the cafeteria at his London office. Kate appeared shortly afterwards holding two mugs of double-shot Americanos.

'Congratulations on your promotion,' she said. 'Looks as though our mysterious Marc Sentus did the job.'

'Thanks, Kate. Yes, can't deny that. Took me by surprise. Now I've got to stand up there tonight with all those other winners at our annual UK awards ceremony.'

'Winner takes it all! Well, at least you won't be nervous giving your acceptance speech. You did a good job on your final evening over in Manhattan,' Kate replied, smiling broadly. 'Something no doubt to do with that session over there when he discussed public speaking with us.'

'Yes, definitely that, amongst other things,' Jon replied.

'Oh, hi, Jon. Do you mind if I have this seat?' asked Tom, a colleague from the IT office in Oxford. 'It should be a good ceremony tonight. And congrats to you as well.'

'Thanks. Can I introduce you to Kate? She was one of the first people I met over in New York. She's doing the reverse – she's over here for six months.'

'Pleased to meet you, Kate. The view's not as good for you as Central Park, I bet,' said Tom.

'Oh, I'm happy to be here. Like most New Yorkers, I love London,' said Kate. 'I'm originally from Boston.'

'Good old New England!' Tom replied.

'Hey, Jon. How are you doing?' Matthew burst through the double doors with Courteney, caught sight of his former work colleague and shook his hand. 'I'll give the praise later this evening at the awards ceremony. And' – gesturing towards her – 'would this be the famous Kate we read about in the newsletter?'

'Yes. Kate, this is Matthew and Courteney. We worked in the same section for five years. Matthew was jealous of my secondment over in the Big Apple!'

'It certainly didn't do you any harm, Jon,' he replied.

An excited Jennifer walked in, smiling and looking a little bemused as she dumped her coffee mug on the table in front of the sofa.

'What's got to you?' asked Courteney. 'What's with that strange look on your face?'

'Well. You know I kind of get a bit low sometimes,' said Jennifer. 'I doubt myself. I anticipate disaster around the corner.'

'Don't we all?' replied Courteney.

'Of course we do, but my point is I was just flicking through a book on the train this morning and it got me thinking about the power of wise quotes. They can turn a person's life around. It's just amazing.'

'That's it?' asked Courteney, noticing that Jennifer was now settling into 'gazing-up-at-the-ceiling-wistfully' mode. 'You're not going to share anything else with us?'

Jennifer shook herself out of her self-imposed trance. She dragged up her coat, which had fallen over her feet and under the sofa, and produced a scrap of paper from the side pocket. 'Here. I jotted it down. I'll read it out to you. "The world is full of magic things, patiently waiting for our senses to grow sharper." It's attributed to W.B. Yeats.'

Silence fell as they all absorbed the words. Jon looked over to Kate, smiled and then addressed Jennifer. 'I know what you mean. We – I think I'm speaking for Kate too – met somebody over in New York who told us something that shaped our whole idea about life.

'It was a magician we met at the company's gathering. That's where I met Kate for the first time.' Jon pointed towards Kate, seated opposite. 'He gave us this quote. I keep it in my wallet now, as a reminder. Here it is. It's the words of the Stoic philosopher Epictetus: "Man is disturbed not by things, but by the views he takes of them".'

Matthew looked quizzical. 'I may be getting this wrong, but how can some things that disturb you or cause you problems be *your* fault?'

'OK, Matthew,' replied Jon. 'We all have what are termed automatic thoughts. A situation presents itself which dictates our thoughts and then our emotions. It's those thoughts that play the biggest part in determining how we feel about the situation.'

'So how does that help me in a frustrating situation like this morning?' Matthew asked. 'The train was fifteen minutes late and then, in addition to that, a signal failure coming in meant it just stopped on the track for twenty-five minutes. Missed my first meeting.'

'How did you feel during all this?' replied Jon.

'I was agitated, I complained to the on-board steward and the whole time I was rehearsing in my head the letter I was going to write to the chief executive of the train company.'

'Did you notice how some other people in the train carriage were reacting?' Jon asked.

'Yes. Some were on their laptops; others were writing things; some were on the phone; others were reading newspapers and magazines.'

'Were they calm?' interjected Kate, who knew exactly the point that Jon was about to illustrate to Matthew.

'Yes, Kate, most of them seemed calm – or at least more in control than I was, I suppose,' he replied.

'So, Matthew, you and your fellow passengers were all in the same situation and it seems you chose a different way to view things,' said Jon. 'Those thoughts affected both your mood and behaviour.'

'I suppose,' Matthew replied, nodding.

Jon then turned his attention to Jennifer as he noticed her smiling and looking as though she wanted to say something. 'Make sense, Jennifer?'

'Yes. Absolutely. I get it,' she replied.

'So, in essence,' Jon continued, 'we are in control of our thoughts. It's our beliefs that dictate how we respond to a situation. The idea that thinking in a different way to change your viewpoint makes you *feel* differently – and therefore leads to you *behaving* in a different way – is a big success story these days. It's the essence of cognitive therapies.

'Our thinking is responsible for everything. Worry, anxiety, fear, joy. A week later, Kate and I met a chap from another floor of the building in the restaurant area. He was exceptionally helpful in explaining to us how our thinking – in particular our self-talk – is the key to everything in life. In fact, if it wasn't for him, I wouldn't be picking up an award tonight.'

'Can you tell us more?' said Tom, intrigued, as he looked at the others gathered around the table.

'Well, gladly. Whoever wants to stay is welcome. This is starting to look like a scene from *Friends*!' said Jon, pulling his chair closer to the sofa. 'Just be assured – I'll be there for you!'

'I'll get some more coffee,' said Kate. 'This is going to take a while. Don't wait, Jon; start the story. It's OK. *I was there!*'

Jon smiled. 'Anyway. It started at the company's evening get-together over in a hotel on 6th Avenue. I'd only been in town for a week. I was sauntering around, looking lost, spilling a large glass of Chardonnay that I'd just taken from a tray. It all began then ...'

*... I wandered into one of the other rooms. A smartly dressed man in a tuxedo waved over to me. He was holding a pack of cards.*

'Good evening,' I said as I approached him.

'Hi, I'm Scott,' he replied, beckoning me to sit down by his small table. 'Your company's hired me as the magician for this drinks reception slot. Your accent tells me you might be from across the water, is that right?'

'Yes, I'm from the London office,' I said. 'I'm here for six months. My name's Jon.'

'First time in New York?'

'Yes. Exciting,' I said. 'Feel as though I've been here a thousand times after seeing it in films and on television.'

'Well, this city is a magical place, I'm sure you'll find. Like nowhere else.'

A woman walked into the room holding a bottle of Coke in one hand and struggling to eat a petit four. Scott beckoned her over.

'Hi there. Grab a seat. Then you might stand a chance of that reaching your mouth,' Scott joked.

'Oh, thanks a lot. These don't help,' she said, pointing to her high heels and laughing. 'My prime-time TV news anchor stilettos. My trainers are in my bag downstairs – I thought I'd try and look sophisticated for this evening. Meeting all these new faces from different offices. I'm Kate, by the way. Hi.'

'Hi, Kate. My name's Scott. I'm the magician for this evening. Have you met Jon from London?' he said, pointing over to me.

'No, I haven't. Pleased to meet you, Jon. How are you settling in?'

'Well, it's early days yet,' I said to her. 'Been here a week now. I'm hoping to pick up some good experience and motivate myself to get some of that confidence I see in a lot of people here. How long have you been with the company?'

'Oh, I moved from the Boston office just over a month ago,' she said. 'My boss here said to me if I do well, he'd let me transfer over to somewhere in Europe.'

A bell sounded, followed by an announcement. 'The drinks bar will be closing in half an hour.'

'I don't want to monopolise you,' Scott said to us, 'but can I quickly show you some card magic before you go?'

I nodded and Kate said, 'Great. I love magic.'

He asked the two of us to look at a deck of cards and to choose one. Scott then asked Kate to look at the card that was in an envelope that had been on the table the whole time. She took it out of the envelope and turned it over.

'Is that your card?' Scott asked.

I can remember Kate putting her hand over her mouth as she spoke – 'Oh my God' – and I shook my head in amazement.

'I know it must get boring for you to hear this,' I said to him, 'but how did you do that?'

'I can tell you. As magicians we bend reality. The magic happens in the spectator's mind. We change people's perceptions – so nothing is as it seems.'

'You still haven't told us how you did it,' I said, smiling, knowing it was a futile question to ask a magician.

'I can tell you that your thinking is responsible for everything in life – it creates your perceptions, which in turn create your reality,' Scott said. 'You mentioned earlier you were hoping to motivate yourself to become more confident like some of the people you've met here. You know the secret of becoming confident and successful in all areas of life?'

I remember shaking my head.

'Well, it's to become more aware of how you think. Don't believe everything you think,' he said. 'Your thinking is responsible for how you feel and then ultimately how you behave.'

Scott stood up, aware that he might be detaining us. 'Look, we were just playing around with cards a moment ago. Life is like a game of cards,' he said. 'You take the hand you're dealt at any moment in time and you decide how to play it. When you correct dysfunctional thinking that may be holding you back, this leads to a perception change. A belief change. You can then make things happen – in fact, magic happens.'

*He then showed Kate the underside of the wristband on his right arm, which was inscribed with the two words 'magic happens'.*

*'Before you go I'd like to give you something that's more than two thousand years old.' He handed us a slip of paper, which we unfolded eagerly. It was a quote: 'The happiness of your life depends on the quality of your thoughts.'*

*'Have you heard of the philosophers, the Stoics?' Scott asked.*

*'Yes,' Kate said. 'That Greco-Roman philosophy they were responsible for. Their ideas are being adopted more and more these days, I remember reading in* Time *magazine there's been a resurgence of interest in them in recent years.'*

*'Quite so. And with good reason,' he replied, I remember vividly. Then he turned to me. 'Good to meet you both.'*

*'I could do with a Stoic to help me learn how to deal with life,' I said jokingly. Then he held out his hand to me and, after delivering a bone-crunching handshake, said, 'I'm sure when the time is right someone will be there to give you the help you need.'*

*'Can I get you another gin, Scott, before the bar closes?' I asked.*

*'No thanks. I'm trying to change my ways,' he said. 'In the past a drink used to be my answer to coping with stress sometimes. It was OK in moderation but it was tempting to keep going, especially at functions and events.'*

*I nodded my understanding. Then he said, 'As a matter of fact – I don't know if you saw the film – they nicknamed me "the Exorcist"...'*

*We looked at him quizzically as he walked towards the door. Then he turned around to us and added, with a smile, '... because I wouldn't leave until all the spirits had gone.'*

'So that was really the beginning of a strange journey which changed our lives,' Jon said. Kate arrived with a tray full of cups of coffee. 'Would you agree, Kate, that it changed our lives?'

Kate nodded and smiled at the group. 'That's an understatement.'

'A question, Jon,' said Jennifer. 'What did he mean when he said to you, "I'm sure when the time is right someone will be there to give you the help you need"?'

Jon looked over to Kate to see if she wanted to answer.

'Well, a strange thing happened not long after. I was with Jon having lunch in the restaurant on the 14th floor of our building in Lower Manhattan. A man asked if he could share our table and we got talking to him. He introduced himself as Marc Sentus, and said he worked in the neighbouring tower in "communications".'

Jon jumped in, 'Yes, and he mentioned he was trialling a talk he wanted to do on how to live a better life by changing your "inner" world.'

'That's right,' Kate added. 'He was talking about controlling your "inner talk" to change your attitudes and emotions. Your feelings, in other words. How it then changes your behaviour.'

Jon said, 'I told him that it was strange because we'd recently met somebody who had mentioned something similar.'

'Yes,' said Kate, 'I asked if he knew Scott, the magician. He was hesitant and didn't comment. I told Marc how the magician had spoken about the cards we're all dealt in life and how we can look at circumstances and question, "Is that your card?" to see how our beliefs may prevent us from looking at things in another way.

'"Thank you, Kate," he then said to me, "I believe you've just given me a *title* for the first session." Then he asked if Jon and I would be interested in joining him for some lunchtime sessions – just the two of us – as a "dry run" for his talk. "Won't cost you a dollar," he said.'

'We were intrigued,' said Jon. 'And I said to Kate if she was game for it, I'd like to give it a go. I certainly suffered from an overactive and racing mind and I'd wondered how much of my stress was self-induced.'

'Yes,' Kate agreed, 'and I suffered from bouts of anxiety at times, and often experienced imposter syndrome.'

'Imposter syndrome? Not *another* syndrome!' said Courteney, looking excited at the prospect of a good story. 'So what happened? Did you go for these sessions?'

'Well, you know what?' said Jon. 'We did. They were held in a vacant room at the back of the restaurant area. At the end of each session we'd have a coffee, and Marc shared a story with us each time and answered any questions we had. And, thankfully, we made an audio recording of each of the seven sessions.'

Jennifer interjected. 'Can we hear them? Have you still got them?'

'As it happens, Kate made a transcript of each individual session,' said Jon. He looked over to Kate. 'What do you think? We've got time, I suppose.'

'We don't need to leave for King's Cross station till 3.30 to catch the train for the ceremony,' Kate replied.

'Shall we make copies and then they can each read through the sessions?' Jon replied.

'Sure. I'll just go over to the 10th and quickly print four copies,' said Kate, disappearing through the double doors.

'So, I guess,' said Jennifer, 'that what you're saying is that self-awareness of your thoughts combined with challenging your unhelpful thinking can change your life.'

'Yes, very much so,' replied Jon. 'It's all in the thinking. When you face adverse circumstances in your life on a day-to-day level or you feel that you were born with a "poor hand", your thoughts will dictate how resilient you are in changing your circumstances for the better.'

'Is it possible to change your way of thinking just like that?' said Matthew.

'Well no, it's not as simple as that. We develop a habit in the way that we think and we let the mind control us, most of the time. But it is possible to stand back and look at the way you're thinking, and change your attitude and previously unhelpful beliefs.'

'But it can't happen overnight, can it?' said Jennifer.

'No, of course, absolutely not. Eventually, you eradicate those "faulty" thinking habits that don't serve you well. Then your brain does the rest with its rewiring, so to speak. Have you ever heard the term "neuroplasticity"?'

Courtney chipped in. 'Yes, that's so encouraging, isn't it? It was thought that the brain couldn't regenerate, but now we know that it creates new connections and strengthens pathways. The research shows that our brain's structure changes based on our experiences and even just from our thoughts.'

'Yes, it's amazing,' said Jon. 'Most of the conversations we have in our life are with ourselves. Our brains move on from the internal "chat" we all engage in, as this mental activity results in a change of structure and circuitry of the brain as new habits form.

'These new pathways can promote well-being and help us develop better attitudes towards adversity, which in turn helps us develop resilience and optimism. That's why we've witnessed the success of cognitive therapies as the most effective and widely practised evidence-based therapy that's in use today.'

Kate burst through the doors holding a sheaf of papers, looking pleased with herself. 'Got them here. A set for each of you.'

'Let's start from Session 1,' said Jon. 'I'm just going upstairs to my office. Need to put the finishing touches on my speech for tonight. Tell us what you think later. I'll be back down in about couple of hours for the next caffeine fix. See you then.'

'I'll head on upstairs too,' said Kate. 'Be back later. Keep our seats!'

# Is That Your Card?

## It's the stories we tell ourselves

*The happiness of your life depends upon the quality of your thoughts.*
*MEDITATIONS* MARCUS AURELIUS (*C.* AD 171–5)

It's often been said that – more than education, more than training, more than experience – it's the level of mental resilience that decides who succeeds in experiencing a satisfactory life. The power to change your life is not so much in your own hands – it's in your head.

In short, we give our thoughts an immense amount of power over the way we live our lives. Our self-talk is responsible for changing our emotional states, moment by moment – and it does so in both positive and negative ways.

We've all come across or read about those lucky people who seem to have been given every advantage in life and yet appear to be unable to translate that into success in any field as they destroy their chances of fulfilment.

Then we see those people who start off in adverse circumstances – and have to deal with a litany of obstacles along the way – yet seem to make something of life. Their self-talk is usually focused on thoughts of optimism. It doesn't mean they don't have negative thoughts – research shows we have between twelve thousand and sixty thousand thoughts every day, with about 80 per cent being negative – but they know that external forces do not have to control their thoughts and emotions.

**It is the conversation we have with ourselves that creates our feelings.**

Many of us will recognise the following statement, so often part of a running commentary in our mind: 'I'll never be able to do that.' Suppose it was changed to: 'I'll do my best, and see what happens . . .' It won't have escaped you that this second statement has no negative undertones.

The English novelist Rudyard Kipling got it right when he said: 'Words are, of course, the most powerful drug used by mankind.' With all the brain research available to us now, neuroscientists have proven what he instinctively thought. Our words are responsible for producing emotions that in turn affect the neurochemistry of our brain.

We need to keep reminding ourselves that words carry tremendous power. They are responsible for shaping our thoughts and our emotions. Our ability to cope, to handle the 'slings and arrows' of everyday existence, are dependent on the stories we tell ourselves as we try and do something with the cards we are dealt, resulting, sometimes, in feelings of hope or despair.

Our life is very much like being part of a card game as we come to terms with what we are born into, the situations we face and how we play those cards. You'll hear the expression: 'The luck is in the cards, the skill is in the player.' As in a game of poker, the different situations we face are the hands that we are dealt by chance. We don't have any choice in what we will be dealt; it's what we do with the cards that makes the difference.

A lot can be learned from observing a game of cards. How a bluff can change your unfavourable hand simply by presenting a change of attitude or thinking. Chance plays a big part in life, just as it does in a card game. We can't control what happens to us, but we can choose how we handle the situation on a daily basis.

How often do we find that, just as we're 'getting on with life' with a certain amount of acceptance and coping strategies, out of the blue we find ourselves dealt a card or a hand of cards that plunges us into a state of anxiety and stress?

We have to play the cards we are dealt. Of course, it's frustrating to see other people who may have had better luck. Their 'royal flush' compared with your bust hand. So change the story and look for the more favourable elements of your life.

You may have had unhelpful and tragic 'cards' – perhaps you experienced a less-than-idyllic childhood – but that doesn't need to define you. The opportunities and lifestyle that people are born into are so varied. We've all come across people who don't seem to have enviable cards yet manage to cope with testing situations and crises as they arise – and become stronger as a result when dealing with future adversities.

Then we see others collapse in the face of adversity and suffer a lifelong negative reaction to their experiences. Of course, any individual's experience of failure, sorrow or trauma is very real to them and is not something that can be casually dismissed.

So we have a situation with one person being able to 'bounce' back from a difficult situation or setback, while another may dwell on it for a long time. Two different and long-lasting effects on two different individuals. The reason for this? Their thinking.

Ancient philosophers made us aware that there are certain things in life we are unable to control. As such we should stop causing ourselves unnecessary suffering by trying to control those things that are beyond our capability.

Much of life's unhappiness derives from thinking we can control things that are actually beyond our control. We should put our emphasis on those things that we're able to control and accept the rest as it happens to us. Arguing with reality and wishing that things were different did not function within Stoic philosophy (we'll discuss this in Session 3).

In all the sessions, we'll be talking about taking responsibility for the way we view situations and therefore our emotional response. This will show you how powerful your inner state is in improving your mental well-being. It frees you from needing to change a circumstance or other people in order to feel better.

We all have our specific goals and aspirations, and what we believe about them will determine how we feel and behave. We're all responsible for shaping our own reality. Somebody once said, 'If you don't imagine, nothing ever happens.' The American film director Steven Spielberg remarked, 'My problem is I can't turn off my imagination.'

So, to get to the central point that relates to everything we'll be discussing in these sessions, how we *think* about things determines how we *feel*, which determines how we *act*. It's hugely empowering for people when they become aware that when we control our thinking, we can change our life – and we improve our mental health.

We can look at society and see in the worlds of business, sport, entertainment, politics and in everyday life the stories of those people who, despite unfavourable circumstances, followed their dream. Fuelled by this urge and desire they go on to make things happen. They engage in thinking that, despite failure and 'roadblocks' along the way, fosters their self-belief and self-confidence.

It is our self-talk that influences our activity and success (or lack of it). So we don't get what we *want* in life. We get what we *expect*. If those two happen to match, that's all well and good.

## We are all storytellers

Our lives are in effect a story that is being created moment by moment. We, as humans, construct reality from the stories that we tell ourselves. It becomes the narrative of our life and dictates the parameters for our achievements. We tend to focus on what is happening in the 'external' world and pay scant regard to what's actually happening in the 'inner' world of our mind.

In other words things happen, you tell yourself a story about why it happened ('I'm not bright enough to master this'; 'I'll never get picked for promotion, I'm too . . .'; 'I'm much too old for . . .') and it becomes fact. When we stop to analyse and examine that inner talk we can challenge the 'evidence' for our thinking, engage in more rational thought and craft better stories.

Your life reflects the image of your thoughts. The novel that you pick up from the shelf is narrated to explain what is happening. We do the same with our lives. Our self-talk describes to us what is happening. More importantly, it describes the world *as we see it*.

In our lifetime we're all faced with the past, the present and the future. We have the cards that we were dealt from an early age and so our past exerts a considerable influence on us. From our activities and those early 'slings and arrows' we build up an experience bank, which is comprised of all the situations, memories and emotional experiences we've faced or felt – all of which play a big part in how we interpret events and make decisions in the future.

But this may be holding you back. You may be telling yourself stories from a script that involved early financial deprivation or sibling conflict or feelings of diminished worth in the family hierarchy or educational inadequacy. So pay attention and re-examine the narrative.

We all tread a different path in life and our individual stories can never be the same as anyone else's. Our attitudes, beliefs and the ways in which we perceive the world are unique.

Our stories become our truths. Because of this it is difficult to alter our long-standing beliefs, which – in the main – can be negative in nature, causing us recurring problems with our mental health. But always remember that there are three sides to every story – yours, mine and the truth.

## Mental health awareness

Mainstream media is much more open about discussing mental health these days. Of course, it's a problem for the whole of society and for people of all ages. Lately, it's been highlighted how more and more young people are seeking help for problems ranging from anxiety and depression to lack of self-esteem. Social media, it's been repeatedly said, has exacerbated the situation. As one commentator noted: 'We're in an age when it feels as though children have only two states of being: asleep or online.'

Experts have for years been saying that mental health literacy should be a core competency by the time we reach the end of our school and university days. Children and adolescents would benefit hugely and feel empowered by being taught that, in most situations, they have control over their *thoughts* and *feelings*. It's important that children develop a certain amount of mental flexibility and toughness instead of, perhaps, having parents and family constantly trying to spare and protect them. If they don't develop this capacity in childhood, it's not miraculously going to happen when they reach further education.

So if they do go on to graduate education, and don't develop it there, they'll face further problems in the future. Think about those job applicants who are successful, join organisations and then encounter problems when the going gets tough. What stories are they telling themselves to help them face challenges? Many people believe that a mental health 'pandemic' has been around for many years. If children and adolescents were taught that they are in charge of their thoughts and feelings, and that they have an element of control in the circumstances they face, this would lead to a feeling of empowerment.

The present is the here and now. It is only now that we can make any changes. If you want to change how things are and you have a vision for the future, you need to adopt a thinking pattern that helps you towards your goals and negates your doubts and fears. The stories we create about our experiences have the power to instil in us feelings of optimism, hope, joy and elation or feelings of pessimism, desperation, sadness and hopelessness.

**The story you tell yourself can spur you on – or can hold you back.**

### Don't believe everything you think

Let's just analyse why thinking is so different from our senses. Our senses are related to present-moment experiences. For example, you can't smell something or taste something in the future or in the past. But when it comes to thinking we're not restricted to what's happening at this very moment. We set ourselves up for sadness, disappointment, anger and other feelings because we are able to change our perspective and broaden things away from how things 'are' to:

- How things 'should' be;

- How they 'used' to be;

- How we're afraid they might be in the future (we're introducing some anxiety/fear here).

Easier said than done, maybe, but if we're able to develop an acceptance of what's happening in life – as opposed to always wishing and insisting that things *should* have turned out a different way – we spend less of our precious time experiencing angst and being in a stressful state.

You can look at your thoughts as representing the personal interpretations and perceptions of how you understand what's happening in situations in your life. The internal process that gives meaning to events. It's inevitable that the way we construct reality will be shaped by our beliefs and opinions, and this in turn will have an effect on how we see *ourselves*, *other people* and the *world*.

In short: **if you want to change your life start with the way you talk to yourself**.

It's easy and quite natural to want to blame situations and adversities and other people for causing us stress, anxiety, frustration and anger as we try to get on with day-to-day living. But we become what we think. The mind is perfectly capable and perfectly willing to hold us back. Or it can do the opposite.

It's our thinking that determines how we choose to view our situation, which decides how we see the world and its opportunities. Sometimes it takes losing something for us to realise that our unhappiness or dissatisfaction is purely because of our thinking. To help explain this, I'd like to recount a tale to you.

*There was a King who was very wealthy. He had luxurious palaces, servants and the best of everything. The best food, the best clothes, the best jewellery.*

*Despite all of this he was unhappy.*

*He turned to alcohol and engaged in other pleasurable and self-destructive behaviours. But happiness was still beyond him.*

*He put up a notice offering a reward to any person who could show him how to feel happy.*

*Hundreds of people visited and tried in vain for him to experience this emotion. They all failed. One day a wise Sage showed up and asked to meet the King privately.*

*The King recounted his problems to the Sage, who then asked him: 'Are you absolutely sure in your mind that you would be willing to make any sacrifice in order to achieve a state of happiness?'*

*The King assured him: 'Any sacrifice whatsoever in order to find happiness.'*

*The Sage then explained that happiness was not necessarily found in possessions. Would he be willing to give up all his wealth? That, the Sage said, could make him truly happy.*

*The desperate King said he would do anything that he was advised. He gathered all his valuables of gold, silver and jewels, put them in a chest and had his servants place it in front of him.*

*'Are these definitely all of the valuables you have?' the Sage asked. 'Because it's important you give everything.'*

*The King assured him that these were all the valuables and that he also owned land and palaces, which he was willing to leave behind.*

*'What is it I have to do now?' he asked.*

*'Take a few breaths and close your eyes for a few minutes,' the Sage replied.*

*When the King closed his eyes the Sage picked up the chest of valuables and started to run away. The King, realising he had been duped, stood up and his feelings of unhappiness quickly changed to anger. He started to chase the Sage, shouting, 'You cheat! You* scoundrel! You've cheated me, you charlatan, you're probably not even a Sage!'

The Sage eventually reached a narrow alley and hid there. After fifteen minutes or so of searching, a servant told the King they had seen a man carrying a small chest going into the alley. He confronted the Sage.

He shouted at him, 'You're nothing but a common thief. A Sage you pretended to be. You came here under false pretences, not to teach me how to obtain happiness; all you wanted to do was steal my wealth.'

The Sage looked at the King and with a wry smile on his face asked: 'Tell me. Are you happy that you've recovered your chest of gold, silver and jewels from the cheating scoundrel Sage?'

'Yes,' the King replied.

'Sit down.' He beckoned to the King as he ushered him to sit opposite him on an area of smooth rock.

'Can't you see? I've just given you a magic formula for how to obtain happiness.'

'What do you mean?' the King replied.

'Just think about it. Around thirty minutes ago you had all your wealth, all of that silver, gold and jewels. But you were unhappy.'

'Yes.' The King nodded.

'Then I took all this away from you. Now you've got it all back and you're happy'.

The King started to let go of his bemused expression and leaned forward.

The Sage continued, 'So where has this happiness come from. Has it come from the wealth? Or has it come from inside of you because you've achieved something you wanted to achieve?'

The humbled King stood up, bowed to the Sage and expressed his utmost thanks for the lesson he had just been given.

## Be aware of that negative thinking 'bias'

For most of us, it seems that healthy and realistic positive thinking takes a lot of effort, whereas its alternative, counterpart negative thinking – the *'uninvited guest'* – is much easier to handle.

If your early years were spent in a happy and caring environment, then it's more likely – but not guaranteed – that thinking and seeing the world in a positive way will come easier. If early experiences and memories relate to difficult and troubled times, then there will more likely be a tendency towards more negative thinking. This attitude often leads to a self-fulfilling situation where our life and circumstances continue to mirror those negative thoughts.

But we can change all this. A thought has no power other than what you give it. The momentum starts because you keep the same thoughts going. It's often said that the mind is a creature of habit, so it can just as likely entertain positive thoughts continually as it can negative thoughts.

The secret is not to let those unhelpful and self-critical thoughts become entrenched; to be aware of and catch them before they do damage. A negative thought is just that: a negative thought.

As we'll discuss in later sessions, because our feelings are a *consequence* of the way we think, for much of the time we may experience negative emotions. All our emotions come from within – it is what we tell ourselves that creates our feelings.

Everything in life is a story. So if changing your thinking can change your life, then we can say that you can change your story to change your life. The first step is to be aware of those stories we are telling ourselves – every day – about what's happening to us and in the world, how good or bad we are, how other people are behaving. That's quite a lot to get through!

'I don't think I'll go to the gym for my personal trainer appointment this afternoon. Nobody's mentioned I look

leaner or fitter yet. It's a waste of time and money. I'm stuck with this body shape.'
*What? Results after two sessions?!*

'No thanks, Petula. Count me out for the department's weekly raffle. I'm just one of those unlucky people. I never win anything.'
*What? Those three raffle/lottery tickets you've bought in your lifetime?!*

'Think I'll tell finance I've changed my mind about attending that conference and exhibition next month. Last time I went to one of those events I didn't meet any interesting people.'
*What? Are the same people going to be at this event?!*

As human beings we have our own subjective opinion in how we interpret and view the vagaries and challenges of everyday living. This attitude or belief is what determines our individual psychological response to an 'event'. Our thinking determines how we choose to view our situation, which in turn decides how we see the world and its opportunities.

Much research has been done – and we'll cover this later– into how it is our thinking (cognitive) style, and therefore the way that we interpret situations and events, that determines how well we cope with situations.

It's safe to say that all of us struggle with insecurities at one time or another. We can all be accused of fallibility. If we're emotionally healthy we probably have good coping skills to deal with adversity and may manage stress better than most people. All the success that you experience in your life will ultimately be the result of your thoughts – as will much of the failure be too. In other words it's responsible for our emotions. So, for much of the time it's this self-talk that's driving our emotions.

So, to get to the central point that relates to everything we'll be discussing in these sessions: **how we *think* about things determines how we *feel*.**

It really is as simple as that.

## 'Watching' your mind

How many times have you heard people say – or perhaps have said yourself – 'I can't help the way I feel.' Well, it's time to take a fresh look at this. You know now that your *own* thoughts produce a feeling, but you may have been labouring under the delusion that something else, some 'higher power', is preventing you from changing the way you feel.

Your mind is within your control. Just as it creates a particular feeling it also allows us to change that feeling by stepping back and 'watching' our mind.

In other words we can *dispute* our own thinking.

How we think about something affects how we feel both emotionally and physically. It's the mind–body connection at work. Your thinking *creates* the emotions you feel. You need to prove this to yourself before we progress to the next session, so try this simple exercise:

- Decide on an emotion you want to feel: for example, anger, sadness, guilt, nervousness or joy.

- Now try feeling this emotion *without* thinking of a situation that brings forth these feelings ...

It's not possible, is it? That makes us very powerful. It means your emotions don't have to have control over you. You can take charge and improve your mood and become mentally stronger. When you label an emotion you're feeling – sad, angry, guilty, nervous, for example – that simple awareness allows you to put a check on how you're perceiving events. You're able to keep watch and analyse your internal chatter, recognising that it will be the precursor to a feeling and then an action (behaviour).

Spend opportune moments in listening to your inner dialogues. Much of the time you'll find that they're critical or negative. These conversations influence how good – or bad – you feel about yourself and how you respond to things that happen to you. It's the perception of our problems that formulates our story.

So powerful are our stories and beliefs that the process of 'watching our mind' (more about that later) is paramount to improving the quality of our life and dealing with all the doubts, fears and adversities that we face. Yet, even when we've trained ourselves to examine our own thinking as it occurs, we will likely come across deeply held beliefs that we had as children, as well as those that have been developed through life's experiences.

Our aspirations or expectations may be stories we've created about what we expect from other people, ourselves and the world. Our thinking may be sending us down the path of disappointment, anger, frustration, envy, anxiety and much more. We all have psychological vulnerabilities that may be ignited by a 'spark' that stems from long-standing beliefs.

When we're upset about a situation or something related to other people it is our attitude or beliefs which formulate our thinking, which in turn is driving our feelings. (We'll talk more about this when we discuss the ABC model in Session 4.) Equally, our feelings – or emotions – can generate unhelpful thoughts about what is happening to us in the moment, or revive unpleasant events from the past or anxieties about what may happen in the future.

The 'cognitive' psychotherapeutic revolution over the last half-century or so has highlighted the idea that we are responsible for generating our thoughts. We are also responsible for changing those thoughts, when appropriate, to a healthier and less irrational viewpoint.

**The conversations that we have with ourselves are the most important ones we will ever have.**

In all the sessions we'll be talking about taking responsibility for the way we view situations and therefore our emotional response. It will show you how powerful your inner state is in improving your mental well-being; it frees you from needing to change a *circumstance* or other *people* in order to feel better.

Because our feelings are a consequence of the way we think, for much of the time we experience negative emotions. Your beliefs – or attitudes – drive your thinking, which in turn affects how you feel and then how you behave. So many of us take thinking for granted and never step back to consider that our *beliefs* are at the heart of everything we do. More importantly you have the power to control your mind, instead of allowing your mind to control you.

We all have our specific goals and aspirations, and what we believe about them will determine how we feel and behave. We're all responsible for shaping our own reality. It's often said: if you don't imagine nothing ever happens.

Which category would you put yourself in?

• Some people *want* it to happen.

• Some *wish* it would happen.

• Others *make* it happen.

So, your experiences and success in life will always be determined by how you play the game.

## COFFEE BREAK

On a flight from Las Vegas to London a lawyer was seated next to a woman in the front section of the plane. The lawyer asked what she had been doing in Las Vegas.

'My son works for one of the hotels. I was visiting him. How about you?'

'I was at a lawyers' convention for six days,' he replied. 'A bit dull to be honest. But I managed to get time for poker and blackjack at the casinos.'

'Slot machines and the occasional Keno – that's my mark,' she replied.

The flight attendant passed by and, looking at the woman, leaned over gently and said: 'Everything OK, Linda? Do you want anything?'

'I'm just a little tired. Need to get some sleep. A glass of water would be fine.'

The attendant then asked the lawyer: 'Anything for you, sir?'

'Double bourbon, no ice. Thanks.'

The lawyer turned to the woman and asked if she'd like to play a little game, a kind of a quiz, just to while away the time. She could get help, he pointed out, from any source. She politely declined, turning towards the window to indicate she needed to take a nap.

The lawyer persisted and told her that it was a fun and easy game. 'I ask you a question and if you don't know the answer, you give me $5. You ask me a question and if I don't know the answer, I give you $5.'

'With all due respect,' she replied politely, 'I don't think this is a game for me. I don't have your education and no doubt the opportunities you have had in your life. Mind you, I have to tell you something that my son told me a couple of days ago, after spending some time working on the gaming tables.

'He said, "A person can be highly educated, professionally successful – *and financially illiterate.*"'

'I dare say,' he replied. 'OK, let's change it a bit. If you don't know the answer, you give *me* $5. If I don't know the answer, I give *you* $500. Is that fair?'

This caught her attention and, thinking she'd get no peace unless she agreed, she turned to face him.

'I just want to get this clear,' she said. 'If you ask *me* a question and I can't give the answer, I pay *you* $5.'

'That's what I said,' he replied.

'If *I* ask you a question,' she continue, 'and *you* can't give me the answer, you pay me $500.'

'That's correct,' the lawyer replied.

'Fine. That seems fair to me,' she said.

The lawyer asked the first question. 'What is the distance from the earth to the moon?'

Without saying a word, the woman reached into her purse for a $5 bill and handed it over to the lawyer.

'OK. Your turn now,' the lawyer said.

The woman asked: 'What creature can go up a hill with three legs and then come down with four legs within fifteen minutes?'

The lawyer reached for his laptop and searched frantically for an answer. Then he sent emails and texts to his friends, relatives and work colleagues, but still no joy. An hour later he woke the woman and reluctantly handed her $500. She reached for her handbag, pulled out her purse, neatly arranged the bills, then said, 'Thank you.'

He waited for the answer. But she only turned back to the

window to get more sleep. The flight attendant passed at that moment and noticed the bemused-looking man. 'Everything OK?' she asked. He nodded to her.

The lawyer, having handed over $500 and still troubled by the question without having received the answer, woke the woman and said, 'Well. I gave you the money. *What's the answer!*'

Without saying a word, the woman took off her eye mask, retrieved her purse, handed the lawyer $5, turned to the window and went back to sleep.

# Psychological Stress and 'Stressors'

## Taking care of your mental health

*Be gentle with yourself. You are a child of the universe,
no less than the trees and the stars. In the noisy
confusion of life, keep peace in your soul.*
*DESIDERATA* MAX EHRMANN (1952)

There's so much talk these days about the word 'stress', which is used as a catch-all description of any negative state that we're experiencing. You must have come across people who are constantly telling you how stressed they are.

> 'I moved house last week – nothing but *stress* with endless boxes to unpack and changing over utilities.'

> 'I've had such a *stressful* month. Report time coming up and I've got to get the car serviced.'

> 'I don't think I can meet up with you at the bridge session tomorrow night. Feel too *stressed*.'

'Stress', 'stressful', 'stressed': words used almost unconsciously. And yet, when you think about your own 'slings and arrows', you may feel that many of the problems you're hearing about from other people sound more like 'life' than 'stress'.

We can make a handy definition here:

- Stress is the *reaction* to demands made upon us.

- Stressors are the events, conditions or circumstances that *trigger* stress.

We all have what are called **'acute stressors'**: the demands that we face and deal with over short periods. The difficulties and obligations of everyday life. From the moment we get out of bed in the morning we have a series of ups and downs to navigate. Our days are punctuated with highs and lows, like ocean waves.

You've got to find a trustworthy plumber and get that boiler fixed. There are roadworks at the next junction and it looks as though a car has broken down – you must stay calm. You need to get that performance review done by the end of the month. The list is endless, and the demands pile up. But the important point is that we do eventually deal with them and so we get back to some form of emotional and physical equilibrium.

Then we have what are termed the **'chronic stressors'**.These are situations that affect us over a length of time. That long period of searching for employment after losing or leaving a previous job. Financial worries. Health concerns. Taking care of family. Marriage and relationship problems.

As we'll see in much depth in a later session, our thinking contributes to much of the stress in our lives. We have 'internal stressors' that arise from our own thoughts. We manage to destroy our tranquillity (as the Stoics would have it: see Session 3) and shatter our world in an instant, all by ourselves. Those negative thoughts produce feelings that leave you feeling stressed, fearful and self-critical.

We're accustomed to hearing that positive thinking is good and that negative thinking is bad, but this is an over-simplification. If your mind is healthy, then we can say that you experience negative emotions. This may sound paradoxical at first. We all experience moments of happiness and sadness and our thoughts will produce those feelings at the time. They provide us with information about how we view circumstances as they occur and what we can do about it.

We have a brain that is geared towards ensuring our survival – dating from prehistoric times – and also detecting threats that can confront us in the external world (or even our inner world) as we respond to a simple thought. Mental health is something that affects all of us. It doesn't stay the same because our circumstances change daily. Awareness is the first step to improving our mental well-being, so that we can recognise that thoughts are just thoughts.

You will remember in Session 1 we spoke about the stories in our head that lead us to a judgement, and then the feelings we experience that lead us to a particular way of behaving as a response.

If we 'replay' a story we can look for the thinking 'errors' (more about those later) that motivated us to behave the way we did.

Being unaware that there is a constant dialogue going on in our heads seems to be the problem for most of us. You're thinking about a certain topic and then your mind drifts to something else that is troubling you. There is a gradual progression as you create this fantasy in your head and become agitated, creating a 'mini movie' of possible outcomes. 'If the dentist says I need to have the tooth out instead of a filling, I'll end up missing that client lunch, I bet they'll then give the contract to someone else; I'll be thought of as unreliable, that's not fair, I worked late and at weekends to ...'

Many years ago, in one of my 'mind control' workshops, one of the delegates, Jane, recounted quite eloquently to the whole group how we human beings think. She described the fantasy that we can create in our head as we pretend that our thoughts are 'real', causing us pain and unnecessary physiological stress as the mind–body connection gets to work. She was able to recount vividly her journey to work one morning:

As Jane makes her way to work in the morning her senses register a parked car with its window left open. The next second her mind flits to a thought about how green her next door neighbour's lawn is looking. She stumbles on a cracked paving stone, then notices the herb garden at the front of the house on the corner, that's just been sold. She sees some rocket growing in a separate pot, which leads her to remember the sandwich she'd told her work colleagues she'd try for lunch one day – 'crayfish and rocket on poppy seed bread' – maybe today, she thinks. Then, as she approaches the train station, the next thought that pops into her head is:

*'If the trains are delayed again due to signal failure, I'll miss the meeting again – George [her manager] will be annoyed. Everybody will think I'm irresponsible. He'll ask someone else to handle the account, even though*

*I set it up years ago. He'll probably pass it over to Simon. They'll try and force me out of the job. I'll have a blazing row with Mrs Potter in Human Resources – she'll be wearing that awful magenta twinset. She's never liked me. She's got anger problems; they don't seem to see it. I know she'll incite me to hit her. They'll have to restrain me after the tussle, pull me by my hair. My skirt will split. Security will be called. They'll ask me to clear out my desk. Mrs Potter will press charges – she's vindictive like that – and I'll end up in court. Maybe I'll spend a short time inside, sharing a cell, that awful prison gown. I couldn't eat with the other inmates. I'm not exercising in that yard; those showers. They smuggle substances and sharp objects. One phone call a day – I just couldn't stand it – I'd have to . . .'*

I'm grateful to Jane for providing us with a vivid 'late-night B movie', all from wondering whether her train might be delayed because of a signal failure. We know that creative people tend to have vivid imaginations and research shows that this can predispose some to anxiety. Of course, it can also serve them well in multiple areas of life. Recall the Steven Spielberg quote: 'My problem is I can't turn off my imagination.'

Two points to note: firstly, as I pointed out to Jane, if her last thought as she approached the train station had been related to that crayfish sandwich, this negative downward spiral may not have occurred; and secondly the train, she told us, was on time! (What a waste of those fight-or-flight stress chemicals.)

This example highlights so well how we think. It also brings to mind the psychologist and psychotherapist Albert Ellis (who we met in the Introduction, and will discuss at length in Session 4), who famously said in one of his Friday Night 'standing room only' workshop sessions (which ran for more than forty years in New York): 'If the Martians ever find out how we human beings think, they'll kill themselves laughing.'

As well as internal stressors that arise purely from our own thoughts, we also have stressors that are classed as external, meaning something that relates to our *senses*. We're subject, each and every one of us, to major life changes and upheavals, financial difficulties, employment problems and relationship difficulties. These are the typical external stressors that we face every day. However, we should be aware that all stressors produce a 'cognitive' result because they become part of your thought evaluation.

There are four areas that are affected when we are tipped over into a stressful state:

- Mental;

- Emotional;

- Physiological;

- Behavioural.

Typically, the way that these four areas manifest themselves in everyday personal and working life is:

- A situation happened;

- This led to me to think X;

- Those thoughts led me to feel Y;

- Those feelings resulted in behaviour Z.

Can you identify with this? It sums up most situations that we probably encounter in everyday life. Some of them lead to positive outcomes, of course. Others may push us into a stressful state.

When we're encountering a stressful event it's normal to feel worried or even fearful, and it's also quite normal to feel more than one thing. Just as when you're facing a challenge, you may feel nervous and at the same time excited about the prospect.

Very rarely is our stress caused by just one stressor, as it is usually cumulative. For most of us, perceived time pressure – without everything else we come across – causes stress and has a negative impact on our emotional well-being. All those endless demands pile up, and you feel the stress turning into anxiety.

A lot of the stress we experience is self-imposed. We live in a society that promotes 'multitasking' as a virtue, regardless of the consequences. We can all recognise these situations: we take on too much, we don't plan ahead, we don't do what we say we will do, we procrastinate, we're careless in our talk, we don't nurture our relationships, our time management (if it can be called that!) is often irresponsible – the list just goes on and on . . . I'll have to stop here, for my own 'time management'.

The result is a toll on our mental health. You get to the point where 'living' is draining the life out of you. It reminds me of the scene in the film *Raiders of the Lost Ark* when Indiana Jones's feisty ex-flame tells him, 'You're not the man I knew ten years ago.' Harrison Ford's reply: 'It's not the years; it's the mileage.'

## Be positive about the negative

We have the capacity to destroy our tranquillity and shatter our world in an instant, all by ourselves, as we engage in critical self-talk. Negative thoughts produce feelings that leave you feeling stressed, fearful and self-critical, all of which play havoc with your mental health.

Of course we suffer less mental angst if we assume that all things will work out well, but this attitude means that we're not thinking of how we *could* deal with adversities that may come our way. If you can visualise possible setbacks and situations, you've planned a solution for when things go off course and you can minimise your stress.

A healthy dose of pessimism – whereby you visualise how you might deal with a less than optimal outcome – allows you to plan and problem-solve, if that's possible, for the worst-case scenario. If you're aware of obstacles that may come along in the future, you're effectively preparing yourself with a Plan B.

We all make plans but, as we know, life will often get in the way. The result is that we suffer with our mental health.

Poor mental health is now talked about with much less embarrassment and fear, both in and out of the workplace. We suffer the complexity of modern life, day-to-day pressures, dealing with the change brought on by pandemics, the inexorable rise of digital technology and much more. For many of us this has led to a feeling of being overwhelmed, with a consequent increase in stress.

Our mental health fluctuates with our changing circumstances. It's helpful to look upon it as a continuum which we can move along depending on what is happening in our lives. Some people prefer to use the term emotional well-being, on the grounds that it has a more positive ring.

However, knowledge dispels fear. More people in all areas of life are more open in discussing their state of mental health. If there is any downside it's when people try to 'medicalise' what are, in fact, quite normal stress reactions to challenging circumstances and setbacks.

There was a time when we only spoke about mental health when something went wrong. Now, it's recognised as normal to be concerned about our mental health just as we've been constantly on alert about our physical health.

According to the World Health Organization: 'Mental health is not just the absence of mental disorder. It is defined as a state of well-being in which every individual realises his or her own potential, can cope with the normal stresses of life, can work productively and fruitfully, and is able to make a contribution to his or her community.'

When we feel 'out of control' in our daily lives, typically this occurs in four main areas:

1. Work

2. Relationship

3. Parenting

4. Money

An interesting point often comes up when asking respondents whether it's the major stressors – 'the big four', as I call them – that cause most disruption in their lives, or the minor everyday ones. Time and time again, it's the small stressors that tip people over into a stressful state: those day-to-day problems that accumulate and wear you out. The roof guttering that's leaking, the lost credit cards, the car crash (not your fault), the central heating boiler that's given up . . . The list is endless. This appears to be because with the more major stressors there is a sense that it's necessary to find a way to get through the problem, and, in some ways, they're almost easier to plan for.

The two types of stress that we are exposed to have been classified as **acute stress** and **chronic stress**.

With acute stress we're exposed to an immediate situation that results in the fight-or-flight response when we face an uncomfortable situation or challenge. After the 'threat' is over, this form of stress passes and the physiological reactions disappear as the body returns to normal.

When we look at chronic stress, we're experiencing everyday stressors on a continual basis. It's the long-term exposure to those acute stressors that occur in our personal and working lives.

Since the assault by these stressors is constant, there's no eventual 'switching off' as with acute stress. The body is in a constant state of disequilibrium as we cope with the hand that we're dealt with in daily situations. The flashing light on the motorway telling us that delays of up to 60 minutes are likely, due to roadworks. The speech you have to give at the upcoming awards ceremony. The lost mobile phone (did you leave it on the shelf in the supermarket? 'My life's on that phone . . .'). That flat tyre on the country road. The gas boiler deciding to pack up on 25 December. The screen on the laptop that keeps getting frozen.

You see people shouting at things almost uncontrollably as though it will make any difference, causing themselves even more stress and depleting their energy. I think P. J. O'Rourke, the American satirist and host, put it perfectly when he said: 'Never pick a fight with an inanimate object.'

## It's all about perception

Like it or not, shouldn't we accept the fact that this life of ours is inevitably – fragile human beings that we are – going to assault us with what we classify as stressors on a daily basis? The answer is probably 'yes', if we look at it in a philosophical way.

Are all those relentless emergencies and deadlines that are thrust upon us being classified in the right way? Could a lot of this depend on our attitude? In other words, could we handle the same situations better by *reacting* differently? By thinking in a different way? After all, we know that our behaviour is governed by our thoughts.

When you see people who appear quite placid during what might be classified as 'stressful' situations, you may be intrigued as to how they remain in that state of calm. You, by contrast, may experience uncomfortable and unhealthy emotions.

What are they doing that you're not?

Perhaps the difference might be found if we focus on what *you* are doing? You are thinking – and, more importantly, believing – negative self-limiting thoughts. So it's back to beliefs.

If we become aware of one fundamental thing – that *you* control your mind (and therefore your thinking) and the *mind* doesn't control you, it means that you can change your irrational self-talk. (We'll be discussing this in Session 5.) A change of thinking leads to a change of outcome.

The way in which you react to situations and events may correlate to your exposure to difficult situations in your early life. Personality also has a bearing on an individual's threshold for coping with uncomfortable situations. Analysis of different individuals shows that some people 'downgrade' what others regard as a stressful situation to a healthier one that promotes better well-being: *pressure*. ('Can't talk, I'm under pressure at the moment…') But for some people this very same pressure would still be regarded as stress.

A lot of the time those people who are experiencing 'pressure' regard it as a positive situation. This is because whether at work or in other areas of life, it can act as a motivator. It may challenge us to become more creative, complete a task or find a solution to a problem. But even for those who adopt this more forgiving analysis, there can come a time when pressure becomes excessive. This can tip us over into a stressful state. What may follow is a perception of a loss of control and the feeling of not being able to cope with all the demands that are looming over us.

So we have a problem in defining stress when we consider that what is regarded as a stressful situation will vary greatly for each and every one of us.

The difference is purely down to one of perception. This is highlighted when you consider this definition of a stressful situation: **a situation in which a person perceives that the demands made upon them exceed their ability to cope**.

Therefore it's all down to the way we think, since how we perceive a situation influences the feeling or emotion we experience.

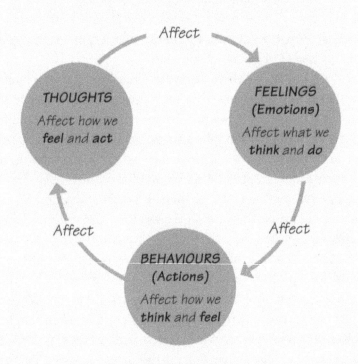

**Our Thoughts, Feelings and Behaviours:**

Of course, sometimes we are alerting ourselves to a 'threat' and our feelings or emotions provide us with a warning system for us to take action as necessary. But we also engage in irrational thinking which distorts our evaluation about events or a person's behaviour. This sets off a process of negative stressful thoughts.

'They're all drifting in late,' thinks Sean. 'It says my talk starts at 9.30am on the itinerary. There were only ten people seated here at that time. Now it's 9.45 and six people have just come in. Oh, and now there's another three. They obviously are not interested in being here, otherwise they wouldn't stroll in late. Perhaps somebody has said something about my previous talks. Boring. Hard-going. Dull as ditch water. Who knows? Why do I bother?'

Well, if Sean had enquired, no doubt some of the delegates would have informed him that there was a twenty-four-hour strike by taxi drivers over at the station so they had to walk from there instead, causing the delay to the start time. This is an example of an irrational type of thinking distortion, often known as 'all-or-nothing thinking' or 'jumping to conclusions'.

## Signs of stress

The Health and Safety Executive, backed up by continuing scientific research, has identified some common emotional signs and symptoms that may explain changes in attitude or behaviour that indicate stress:

• Feelings of anxiety;

• Feeling depressed;

• Feelings of sadness;

• Touchy/irritable;

• Prone to anger;

• Fatigued/drained of energy.

As we deal with stressful situations we often try to cope by anaesthetising ourselves with pleasurable activities and other things we enjoy – like over-indulgence of food or alcohol. You know how it is – you are confined to the house, because of a worldwide virus, with your 'pandemic hair', and that cocktail hour that keeps creeping forward by an hour … 'Is it time for another Lockdown Martini? Yes, don't mind if I do – no ice.' 'Shall we open another box of all-butter cheese straws? Sure, why not?'

This creates its own problems. The scientist Albert Einstein put it well:

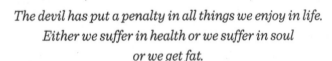

*The devil has put a penalty in all things we enjoy in life.*
*Either we suffer in health or we suffer in soul*
*or we get fat.*
*EINSTEIN: THE LIFE AND TIMES* RONALD W. CLARK (1971)

What about the repercussions of rapidly advancing technology on human social behaviour? Is it any wonder that we're primarily afflicted by stress and negative thinking when all around us the media is focusing on negative events? It's impossible to avoid feeling anxious when we're constantly exposed to footage of wars, floods, famines and natural disasters. It attracts our attention more than uplifting news; this is human nature at work. Wouldn't you agree that it's asking for trouble just watching the six o' clock news?

We need a mindset that can withstand the challenges life throws at us.

Some negative feelings can be classified as healthy in the right circumstances and if they take hold of you for the right amount of time. How is that so?

It's perfectly normal to feel anxious if you're waiting for results after a hospital appointment. Or perhaps you are disappointed at not being shortlisted for the Booker Prize. Angry at the rail company for cancelling services at the last minute. Frustrated at the level of traffic building up in front of you after a breakdown on the motorway.

The important thing about enduring negative emotions is not to try and suppress the feeling altogether, but to moderate the severity of your feelings by *changing your thinking*. Looking on the bright side *all* the time sets us up for disappointment. The positive thinking 'mantra' that you'll often hear other people advocate isn't always the right answer.

We may not be able to control everything that we encounter, but we can do things differently. We can be 'positive' about accepting negative thoughts! We can take every situation and look for a way to try and solve the problem or cope with a setback. If this is not possible, we can change our thinking, which changes the emotions that we are feeling.

It's important to remember that the negative emotions of anxiety, anger, frustration, worry, disappointment and sadness are all a consequence of the human condition. What is crucial to our well-being is the intensity and also the timespan over which we hold on to these emotions.

Seneca, the Stoic philosopher, noted that much of human disturbance is caused by our capacity to be worried about the future or ruminate about the past, and then neglect the present moment, which is most important. He says:

*Wild beasts run away from dangers when they see them. Once they have escaped, they are free of anxiety. But we are tormented by both the future and the past.*
LETTERS FROM A STOIC SENECA (C. AD 65)

## The power of 'no'

We often find that there are people for whom good results and performance at work play a big part in how they evaluate their self-worth, which in turn leads to an improvement in their self-esteem.

It's been found that conscientious workers tend to take on more work with the inevitable result that they become more stressed than their less-willing colleagues. They have trouble saying 'no'. If things go wrong, they become stressed and because their working life is the source of their positive validation, a drop in self-esteem follows.

But we underestimate the power of the word 'no' as a means of improving our mental health. How many times have you come across people who are in a ruffled state because they've said 'yes' to a request and then rue their response as they deal with the pressure and subsequent resentment? More self-induced stress.

Sometimes we agree to something because we're put on the spot – while we're in the middle of something – and we can't, in the heat of the moment, think of the right words for an acceptable refusal. So as a quick option we agree to the request.

More often than not, the mental conflict arises because you're trying to preserve a 'relationship', whether it be a personal or working one. 'They'll be hurt if I say "no".' 'It will look as though I can't cope.' 'If I refuse, she'll be angry with me.' 'He won't like me if I refuse to attend the . . .'

The result is that often we end up resenting our decision as we blame ourselves for taking on the task, and also start to apportion blame to the person who made the request. This can result in angry feelings and then the spiral of negative thoughts begins. All of this because we were unable to summon up a gracious way to convey a 'no' to a friend or colleague. In some cases it may be just a habit of people-pleasing. In many instances it's the actual *word* 'no' that is the problem. So say it in another way that makes you feel more comfortable:

'Thanks for asking me, but I've considered it carefully
and I don't think I'd like to participate.'

'I'm sorry, it's thoughtful of you to think of me, but I
won't be able to contribute to the residents'
association requests.'

'I'd be happy to help you under normal circumstances, but it's a bad time for me, I've been working late as it is.'

'I've decided not to join the committee after careful consideration, as there's too much going on with the children and other family commitments.'

## The mind–body connection and hormones

If we go back to prehistoric times the primary negative emotion would have been the fear response. The stress chemicals switched on the familiar 'fight-or-flight' response. But our modern world has many more lifestyle pressures that constantly assault us.

The brain treats that dreaded moment you feel for your wallet and notice it has been stolen with the same 'danger' as when you unexpectedly stumble across an animal assessing whether the two of you might hit it off over lunch (except you're the lunch!).

The result is a faster heartbeat, shallow breathing, increased oxygen levels, and now we're ready for fleeing or fighting. We're constantly reminded that evolution has provided us with this mechanism to keep us safe. It recognises only safety or potential danger, and it was built for those prehistoric times. This enabled a confrontation with an animal or unfriendly foe (the fight), or the opportunity to be fleet of foot (the flight).

After reaching safety from a bout of fighting or fleeing, the body's parasympathetic nervous system (PNS) would signal to the brain to halt the supply of chemicals. Then the physiological state of the body would gradually return to normal.

Think about when you're watching a re-run of *Halloween* or *Psycho* and each scary scene sets your heart pounding. You know that the stress reaction is being felt in your mind and body. Eventually, it settles down . . . at least until the next fright!

It's worth noting that, from the oesophagus through to the large intestine, the cell lining contains neuropeptides – molecules from our nervous system – and neuropeptide receptors. It's said that the receptors may be the reason why people feel emotions in their gut – the so-called 'gut feeling'.

We have what's called the 'emotional centre' of the brain in the limbic system. Here we have the amygdala, two small almond-like regions of the fear circuit buried deep in this area. It sets off the alarm button when danger or threat lurks. It also contains an important gland called the hypothalamus. Ever been into a high street chemist or pharmacy and asked to speak to the manager? Well, the hypothalamus is the manager of this pharmacy in your brain as it takes decisions as to which chemicals to secrete in response to a thought, or an external situation.

When potential danger is perceived, the amygdala 'makes a phone call' to the hypothalamus, instructing it to activate the fight-or-flight process. The hypothalamus then contacts the pituitary gland asking it to send a message to the adrenal glands (located just above the kidneys) to dispense hormones into the bloodstream. This chain of events is known as the hypothalamus-pituitary-adrenal (HPA) axis.

A number of different hormones are dispensed, but the big two are adrenaline and cortisol. The adrenaline results in a faster heartbeat, which pumps more blood to the muscles (for fighting or running), leading to a rise in blood pressure and faster breathing, which provides more oxygen to the lungs. That's your fight-or-flight response.

The stress hormone cortisol increases the amount of glucose (or sugars) in the blood while at the same time putting a halt to those functions that we don't need during a fight-or-flight situation, like the digestive tract. By putting this in shutdown mode it can provide extra blood for other muscles. With reduced gastric juices in the body our mouth becomes dry due to less saliva. Our breathing becomes more rapid, providing more oxygen to the lungs.

## It's all in the breathing

Breathing well is so important for our mental state. Regular breathing is around twelve to fourteen breaths a minute. If you take some shallow gasps, your body puts itself into anxious mode as if you're preparing for upsetting news or a dangerous situation. Try breathing deeply and slowly – around eight breaths a minute. You should feel more relaxed now as your heartbeat slows.

The problem when we breathe faster or deeper – or both – is that it can result in hyperventilation, which, in essence, is overbreathing. It leads to a loss of carbon dioxide in the blood, which makes matters worse as it distorts the PH balance in the body. This balance is used by the body to regulate our breathing and since it becomes raised it further activates the fight-or-flight response.

This state of overbreathing is typified by what we call upper chest (thoracic) breathing (instead of from the diaphragm, which is better). It occurs when the chest lifts upwards and outwards and the breathing becomes rapid and shallow. Many people with long-term anxiety problems develop this type of breathing as their 'default' mode. The *result*: any time a stressful or anxious situation occurs they instinctively engage in this type of breathing habit. The *problem*: as we've seen there is a chemical change which sets off a chain reaction that prepares us for a crisis.

How can we check whether we are prone to this 'thoracic' habit of overbreathing? Firstly, put your hand on your chest and take a deep breath. Did your hand move? If it did, you're breathing from the thoracic area so you're exhibiting upper chest breathing. The problem: your overbreathing is producing some of those fight-or-flight symptoms – in varying degrees – in your everyday life. Many people spend much of their day, as they cope with perceived threatening situations, breathing from the upper chest. Nothing can change unless their cognition – their thinking – changes.

Therefore, it will come as no surprise that much of the stress and mild anxiety symptoms that people experience in life are exacerbated by their breathing patterns.

Society doesn't help. Many people are influenced by social media and 'celebrity' culture demanding them to look good, to have flat stomachs. The tendency to hold the stomach in and tense the abdominal muscles while sitting, standing or walking – that means all the time – means that diaphragmatic breathing is minimised, in favour of thoracic.

Have you seen those celebrities on the red carpet dressed in their finery, before the Oscars or the BAFTA awards, chatting to interviewers for TV while the paparazzi snap away with their cameras? If we throw in tight-fitting clothes as another negative influence on good breathing, we have even more people unconsciously activating stress chemicals in their body.

We should all be aiming for diaphragmatic breathing. Put your hand on your stomach. Take a deep breath. If your hand moved then you're engaging in this type of breathing. We tend to exhibit this when we're in a relaxed state and also when we're not engaging in any form of physical activity.

This is a healthier way of breathing. It's characterised by slower and deeper breathing. The lower part of the lungs, as they fill with air, push down on the diaphragm. This then causes the abdominal region to protrude and the stomach expands and then contracts, with the rhythm of the breath.

We instinctively veer towards shallow breathing, which can signal to the brain that danger or something untoward is about to happen. In other words we're entering a kind of chicken-and-egg situation. Is my *breathing* causing the stress response, or is it stress that's *causing* my shallow breathing, that's priming my fight-or-flight response?

So changing your *thoughts* will lead to a change in your breathing habits. Equally, changing your *breathing* habits will change your thoughts. Those brain chemicals that cause the stress response will not be activated.

Research shows that at the beginning of a 'threat' (or our perception of a threat), as the body release its stress hormones, the ability to think clearly becomes impaired for about ninety seconds. Our 'executive function' or high-level thinking during that period shuts down.

If we take about a ninety-second break before taking action, the stress hormones that impair our thinking can turn off. This 'pause' when you feel a threat, or when you find yourself in a situation in which you feel anger is building up, is a good policy to adopt. It could be useful for warring couples or parents dealing with stubborn children (maybe less so on a day trip to Jurassic Park).

## Your brain is a pharmacy

You'll remember that our emotions are mediated by the limbic system of our brain with the 'key players' being the hypothalamus (pituitary gland), which is responsible for regulating the hormones in the body, and the amygdala, with its alarm button ready to be activated. This mind–body connection means that our physical state always affects our mental and emotional state.

On the other side of the coin, we can look at the neurochemicals and hormones that promote happiness and increase our sense of well-being: dopamine, serotonin, endorphins and oxytocin.

**Dopamine** is often termed the 'pleasure-and-reward' chemical. When the brain is expecting a reward, dopamine is dispensed as we seek or anticipate pleasure of some sort, and is reinforced when we achieve it. It also steers us to achieve our goals, resulting in happiness. Its effect on mood and pleasure is complemented by the motivation-reward-reinforcement cycle.

It's often dispensed with **serotonin** – the other 'happy hormone'. Being thankful for those things in life that we have can increase our levels of serotonin and regulate our mood (low levels have been associated with depression). It's also responsible for helping to promote higher self-esteem and confidence. Along with another hormone, melatonin, it is also responsible for our sleeping patterns.

Finally, if you're used to exercise, you're probably familiar with **endorphins**, hormones that alleviate stress and pain. They have been described as 'self-produced morphine', and even as 'the laughter chemical', as they are dispensed when we laugh.

These 'feel-good' neurochemicals all help boost levels of our **oxytocin** which increases our sense of affection and helps us bond with others as it increases our sense of well-being.

### How will I cope?

Most of us attempt to handle the challenges we face in similar ways. We'll try and address the 'stressor' until we've fixed the problem or alternatively reduce the stress level to something that we might be able to manage. In psychology we talk of 'coping' strategies that relate to the thoughts and actions we employ in order to manage those 'threatening' situations.

There are two types of coping strategies – 'problem-focused' and 'emotion-focused' – and it's the element of control that decides which strategy we use. Control is not a bad thing, as we'll see in a later session. Having a sense of control is good for our psychological health. If we don't have that feeling of having some control, we naturally feel out of control.

### PROBLEM-FOCUSED COPING

Problem-focused coping involves looking for ways to try and solve the problem. If this isn't possible, we may need to try emotion-focused coping, which is where we change the 'cognitive' aspect, in other words we need to change the emotion (or feeling) that is being experienced. We look for ways to accept 'what is' at the moment and therefore reduce the negative impact that it is having on our lives.

Problem-focused coping is usually present in situations where we can take action to deal with the underlying cause of the stress. If we can change the situation, we may then be able to eliminate the stressor. We make a conscious effort to try to do things to deal with the problem.

Here is an example:

You're spending hours on the phone at work, placing orders for the department. This cuts out a lot of the time that you're able to spend on your other tasks, so you invariably end up working late and therefore have to take a later train. The stress impacts on your tiredness levels and also has an impact on your family life.

Suppose you manage to set up a system with the businesses you deal with, whereby you call another number within the organisation (that you can get through to almost immediately) and you give them the message for the section to call you back as soon as possible to discuss and take your orders. You're taking back some of the control which would help to alleviate the stressor. You reclaim hours of that 'lost' time holding on the phone and consequently rid yourself of the necessity of working late with all the problems it used to cause you.

## EMOTION-FOCUSED COPING

With emotion-focused coping we're dealing with our thinking, as we have to address our feelings and therefore our emotional response to a situation. We do not have direct control over the situation. This may help us to feel better about what is happening to us and gives us a feeling of being better able to handle a situation. This, of course, is essential to improving our mental health. At the same time, since it gives us more clarity in our thinking, it may also help us to explore the possibility of working on problem-focused techniques for the future.

Imagine that your office is relocating to another part of the country. You decide that you can't possibly disrupt your family so you leave your job. It's sad for you, as you had stayed in your organisation mainly because you enjoyed working with your colleagues over the years, with the closeness that had been forged. It takes you a while to come to terms with what is happening, but it forces you to 'reframe' your thinking and take up those opportunities which you'd rejected in the past.

It opens up the possibility of getting in touch with those people who had invited you to discuss opportunities with them if you ever decided to leave your current employment.

You contact some of those organisations and the offer of a new job doesn't take long to materialise. The 'package' is better than your previous job, the travelling time is halved and you're pleased to see how comfortable you feel with your new work colleagues in such a short space of time.

In a way, you can regard this type of coping strategy as treating 'symptoms' as opposed to the actual cause of the stressor. Since we can't change the circumstances, we have to control what is in our power: our *response* to the stressor. Much research has been done in this area and the findings always suggest that those people who engage in emotion-focused strategies are more resilient to stressful situations.

Both Seneca and Epictetus were keen to teach their students the benefits of what Seneca termed *praemeditatio malorum* – 'premeditation of adversity'. In short, they considered this a powerful tool of mental imagery, whereby visualising setbacks or misfortunes helps to prepare for dealing with them by devising coping strategies well in advance.

Being prepared for worst-case scenarios frees the mind of fear and the unknown while at the same time providing a kind of 'shock absorber' when it is needed.

*If you want a man to keep his head when the crisis
comes, you must give him some training before it comes.*
LETTERS FROM A STOIC SENECA (C. AD 65)

Awareness is the first step to improving our mental health, and then we can recognise that thoughts are just thoughts. **If you want to change your life, change the way you talk to yourself.**

There are things we can't change and things that are controllable. This is the essence of our next session, in which we will look at the ancients' way of dealing with stress.

---

## COFFEE BREAK

A man was circling in the air in a hot air balloon and was getting more and more stressed as he realised he was lost.

He started reducing his altitude and spotted a woman walking below. He descended a little more and called out to the woman.

'I say. You couldn't help me, could you? I've promised a friend I would meet him nearly two hours ago, but I don't know where I am.'

The woman looked up at the balloon and shouted out to the man. 'You're in a hot air balloon hovering approximately 40 feet above the ground. You're about 38 to 46 degrees north latitude and between 50 and 54 degrees west longitude.'

'You must be in IT support,' the man replied.

'I am,' the woman replied. 'How did you know?'

'I'll tell you,' the man replied. 'Everything you just informed me about is technical, I've no idea how it can help me

---

and the fact is, I'm no better off because I'm still lost. To be frank, you haven't been much help at all. To make matters worse, you've delayed my trip.'

The woman replied, 'You must be in management.'

'As a matter of fact, I am,' the man replied. 'How did you know?'

'Well, it's quite simple really,' the woman responded. 'You have risen to where you are due to a large quantity of hot air. You don't know where you are or where you are going. You made a promise which you've no idea how to keep and you expect people beneath you to solve your problems. The fact is, you are in exactly the same position as you were before we met – but now, somehow, it's all my fault.'

# The Ancient Philosophy of the Stoics

## What would Epictetus, Seneca and Marcus Aurelius say?

*People who are ignorant of philosophy blame others for their own misfortunes. Those who are beginning to learn philosophy blame themselves. Those who have mastered philosophy blame no one.*
*ENCHIRIDION EPICTETUS (C. AD 125)*

The most important influence of Stoicism today is on psychotherapy, as it was the foundation for the creation of the first form of 'cognitive therapy', rational emotive behaviour therapy (REBT). In essence the Stoics remind us that there are helpful or unhelpful ways of how we can view any situation or problem we encounter.

The first Stoic philosophers lived more than two thousand years ago, during the Greco-Roman period. They belonged to a school of philosophy that started around 300BC, which provided a blueprint for what might now be termed psychological resilience. Their philosophy has enjoyed a resurgence in popularity over recent decades, due to the success of modern-day cognitive therapies (more about that later).

It was in the last century BC that Stoicism produced the 'big three' philosophers who ended up contributing so much to its enduring principles: **Marcus Aurelius** (AD 96–180), the last (and one of the greatest) of the Roman emperors; the Roman statesman **Seneca** (4 BC–AD 65); and the Greek philosopher **Epictetus** (AD 55–135).

Marcus Aurelius was dubbed the philosopher-king. Seneca was a famous playwright and senator who served as an adviser to the Emperor Nero. Epictetus was a former slave and exile who became a teacher. Their writings represent the only surviving Stoic texts, as much was lost during the demise of the Roman Empire. None of their works were intended for publication.

Epictetus taught his *Discourses* to a group of students, almost like a therapy session. The writings of Seneca came principally from the *Letters* he wrote to his student Lucilius, taking on the role of philosophical mentor or therapist.

Marcus Aurelius wrote a personal daily journal during his reign, amidst wars, pandemics, famine and other upheavals. His journal eventually became known as the *Meditations*; its original title was *To Himself*. So we're able to gain access to his thoughts as he searched for Stoic remedies to help him in his everyday life as well as dealing with setbacks and problems as emperor of Rome. This included the Antonine Plague which swept through Rome from AD 165 to 180, killing millions of people.

He was given a copy of Epictetus' *Discourses* and this became his guide for living and shaped his philosophy of life. Echoing the principal message of the teachings of Epictetus, he wrote:

*You have power over your mind – not outside events.*
*Realise this and you will find strength.*
*MEDITATIONS* MARCUS AURELIUS (*C.* AD 171–5)

Their collective writings have been studied over the centuries in the Western world. They've greatly inspired many thinkers, writers, politicians, military personnel, US presidents, business entrepreneurs and, now, due to a resurgence of interest, more and more of us who are looking for a philosophy for daily life. We have to remember, however, that in the translation of these ancient texts there may be some words and phrases that may slightly differ in our modern-day interpretation from their intended meaning.

These ancients had a great interest in human and social psychology as we know it. The value that they put on the understanding of mental wellness and the harmony between the mind and the natural world cannot be overstated.

For them, an observance of their three tenets of logic, acceptance and control is the key to minimising suffering and improving daily well-being.

**Logic** is needed in order to raise self-awareness and identify situations where a person's beliefs are irrational and unrealistic, causing unnecessary negative emotions.

Also key to good living is an **acceptance** of one's circumstances

– and acknowledging that in life there will always be good and bad fortune – while at the same time trying to influence situations and circumstances where possible.

Finally, **control**, which is fundamental to the other two tenets. We must recognise what is within our power to control and what is not, and take note of the distinction. We achieve tranquillity when we accept that a lot of what happens to us is beyond our control. Only by acknowledging and accepting that can we gain peace in life.

The purpose of their teachings was clear: **to help people find a better way to live their lives**.

They formed their philosophy based on the fact that we all have a certain amount of power relating to how we *feel* by changing the way that we *think*. They also felt that if there was no philosophy of how to deal with everyday life, then humans make the mistake of taking the easy option of acting on their impulses and moods.

They encouraged their people to spend time questioning what was really important in life – a life of 'value' or a life of 'valuables'? In addition, they were keen to remind people that a lot of the things that they spent time worrying about were not that important (our modern-day 'stressors') and caused needless adverse emotions. Why trigger that unnecessary fight-or-flight response?

What is fascinating is to see how human nature hasn't changed that much over the millennia; the psychological insights that the Stoics proposed in order to gain a kind of inner 'peace' are as relevant today as they were then. Their ideas feel modern and inspirational, providing a lifelong path to resilience, acceptance and 'mindfulness'.

Over the last few decades, as more and more people have become aware of the need for a sense of direction and purpose in life, there has been a discovery of the Stoic philosophy in providing that 'self-help' to cope with everyday living.

In those ancient times there were no psychologists or

psychiatrists, and philosophers were regarded as 'physicians of the soul'. Who, today, could argue with their principles of:

- How to lead a fulfilling and happy life;

- How we can all become better human beings;

- How we can handle adversity;

- How to be conscious of our emotions;

- How we can master self control.

It is worth noting that there's confusion amongst some people who mistake the lower-case stoic (as opposed to Stoic with a capital 'S'), and believe the word refers to a state of suppressing emotions. The ancient Stoics were totally the opposite as they were perfecting their psychological techniques to prevent negative emotions formulating in the first place.

## The Stoics and control

We know that your emotions follow your thoughts. The Stoic principle is to go a stage further and *prevent* thoughts being formulated by changing your belief patterns. Then they don't become part of the mind–body connection. If you're unable to prevent negative emotions, then they used techniques to challenge them.

According to Epictetus, we have complete control over our beliefs or judgements. But who was he, and what influenced him?

Epictetus was born into slavery around AD 50–60 during the reign of the Emperor Nero. At that time the most intelligent were trained to utilise their talents and given work as teachers and administrators.

After Nero's death, Epictetus was granted his freedom and he set up a school of philosophy, eventually becoming the leading Stoic teacher. His Stoic school was the equivalent of a physician's consulting room. The idea was that the patients (his students) should leave the room feeling bad as opposed to good. What did he mean by that? He felt that treatment given to any patient that would likely cure them would probably also cause them some discomfort.

His message was clear: the main concern of philosophy was the art of living, and the ideal pupil was someone who seeks to be 'tranquil and free from turmoil'.

Epictetus' wisdom survived and is available to us thanks to a student, Arriam, who took notes during his classes. This *Enchiridion (Handbook)* tells us that we have little or no control over things that happen to us (in the *external* world) but we have control over our well-being and happiness (our *internal* world).

We are fortunate to have more of Seneca's writings than either of the other two Stoics, through his essays and also his collection of brief moral letters addressed to Lucilius (*Epistulae Morales*).

He became incredibly wealthy in his lifetime. That did not conflict with Stoic thought as their philosophy taught that there was nothing wrong with enjoying the good things that life has to offer. What was important was the way in which we conduct ourselves and an acceptance and readiness to give up things if circumstances change.

As well as being a successful playwright, he was also involved with politics in first-century Rome as a senator, and later was employed as the tutor and adviser to Emperor Nero (who was not a great employer for promoting employee 'well-being' in the workplace it seems, as he ordered Seneca's death in AD 65).

We have no control over the past and the future. Seneca had this to say:

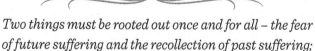

*Two things must be rooted out once and for all – the fear of future suffering and the recollection of past suffering; since the latter no longer concerns me and the former concerns me not yet.*

LETTERS FROM A STOIC SENECA (C. AD 65)

The present, meaning the current moment, is also something over which we have no control as we are experiencing it. Seneca's view was that we waste our time if we engage in worry about the past or future and the present moment. Since this moment is something that we actually have, that we are enduring, if we engage in wishful thinking – about how things could be different – we're wasting the moment. In addition it leaves us dissatisfied.

If we constantly do this then we're destined to live our life feeling disgruntled and dissatisfied. What all three Stoics were saying was that it serves no purpose imagining how things *could* have been better or more preferable than the current moment. It would make the moment we are experiencing less tolerable.

They were keen on citing the phrase *'memento mori'* – 'remember you are mortal' – which inculcates the idea that each day was a gift, to remain in the present and minimise time expended on the trivial. The idea was that we should live life with some meaning and with a sense of urgency:

*Time is the most important thing we have.*

LETTERS FROM A STOIC SENECA (C. AD 65)

The Stoics were mindful of the inner narrative that operates in the background of our minds and is responsible for everything we think, feel, say and do. They were all too aware that the words we use have tremendous power as they evoke an emotional state which results in a specific type of action or behaviour. More importantly they recognised that this both applies to our inner dialogue and also words we use in everyday encounters (our speech).

We can sum up the foundational principles of the Stoics by showing that there were two 'big picture' areas that they were interested in:

## (1) The first foundational principle

Recognising what is within our control and what is not.

The opening lines of Epictetus' handbook, the *Enchiridion*, states: 'Some things are up to us and some are not up to us.' What might appear to be a simple truism is generally considered to be one of the most important and profound statements that survive in the Stoic texts.

*The chief task in life is simply this: to identify and separate matters so that I can say clearly to myself which are externals not under my control and which have to do with the choices I actually control.*
ENCHIRIDION EPICTETUS (*C*. AD 125)

Those 'externals', as Epictetus put it, meant that the external world was not responsible for 'making' you feel the way you do in life's situations. We need to develop an understanding that it is our thinking that determines our feelings and the way we subsequently behave.

It is our mind that creates the thoughts and interpretations of what we come up against, which dictates our internal emotional state.

The philosophy of the Stoics was that we should put our emphasis on those things that we're able to control and accept the rest as it happens to us. It is futile to spend time in life agonising over things over which we have no control. In pursuing 'tranquillity' we have to recognise that there are things we cannot control and develop an acceptance of that and live life accordingly.

Their view was that nature isn't all good or bad. Every human being is the recipient of good *and* bad fortune. Our resilience determines how we cope with adversity. Genetics plays some part in this – someone once remarked to me that the ultimate resilient person would be produced by this formula: resilient parents, a comfortable and secure childhood, sufficient money and education, and tuition that teaches them to regard adversity as a challenge.

So in every circumstance that we face there is an element of control, namely how we *judge* the situation and how we decide to *respond*.

For this reason, the Stoics argued, you could take three people with completely different mindsets: one might be troubled with a situation, another might be untroubled or neutral and the third person might actually be pleased with the circumstances.

## (2) The second foundational principle

Understanding that it is our *thinking* that decides how we view a situation (and the way we subsequently behave).

> *Men are disturbed not by things, but by the view which they take of them.*
> *ENCHIRIDION* EPICTETUS (*c.* AD 125)

This is the other famous and timeless maxim which inspired Albert Ellis's REBT and the creation of cognitive therapies. His

Δ᷅ξλος Επίκτητος γμόμμην.κ;σῶμ' ανάπηρ9ς,
Καὶ πενίω Ι999ς, κϳ φίλος ἀ ϑανάτοις,

Sorcson.delin.                                                      MB fcute

premise was that it isn't the adversities and problems we face in life
that determine our psychological well-being, but our
*interpretations* or judgements that we make of the situations.

In other words, when we observe any event there is no implicit
meaning attached to it and it is our judgements that make it good or

bad. Does this remind you of Shakespeare – who must have absorbed the Stoic principles many centuries later – when he has Hamlet say: 'There is nothing good or bad, but thinking makes it so'?

Announcements in the railway carriage too loud? You feel angry and put it down to the new management of the railway franchise.

Those emotions that you feel are the 'internals'; they are generated by you. The irritants, the loud announcements, are the 'externals'. Your judgement is responsible for how you feel. As Marcus Aurelius puts it:

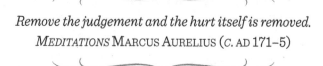

*Remove the judgement and the hurt itself is removed.*
*MEDITATIONS* MARCUS AURELIUS (*C.* AD 171–5)

The foundational principle of Stoicism is that events and people don't upset or disturb us. It's the way we look at these things – in other words our *opinions* or *beliefs* – that dictates what causes us distress in life.

For many people, growing up with instinctive thinking habits as we do, this seems counter-intuitive. Yet, the formation of our beliefs and attitudes is a complicated amalgam of our own personal experiences, observations, assumptions, things that other people have told us and many other influences.

If you develop an acceptance of what's happening in life instead of demanding that things should be different, you spend less of your precious time engaging in angst and feeling frustrated.

The Stoics were very aware of the importance of maintaining good mental health by encouraging a level of self-awareness of managing our own emotions – and also when dealing with other people. They were perhaps the first advocates of what we now term 'emotional intelligence'.

It was the unpredictability of their times that inspired the Stoics to search for ways to deal with things that the world might assail them with, from day to day. By focusing on and controlling their perceptions they felt they could devise practical tools to help themselves deal with any situation.

An acceptance of what was within their power to change and recognition of what was not formed the bedrock of their philosophy. In other words: **accept those things that you cannot change and work to change those things that are within your power to change**. The ancient version of 'don't sweat the small stuff'.

They remind us that our emphasis should be on the one thing that we can control: our thinking. At the same time, they noted the importance of the meaning (our attitudes and beliefs) we attach to events – not the events themselves – that largely determines how we think and react to events.

They were telling us what we know instinctively but what modern-day evidence-based science has confirmed time and time again. Our actions result directly from our thoughts. When:

- We change our **thinking**;

- We change our **feelings**;

- Then we change our **actions (behaviour)**;

- This changes our **life**.

Stoicsim is a practical philosophy for day-to-day living. Epictetus admonished his students in advance:

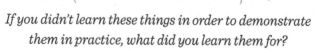

*If you didn't learn these things in order to demonstrate*
*them in practice, what did you learn them for?*
ENCHIRIDION EPICTETUS (C. AD 125)

More than two thousand years later we're still searching for guidance to help us along our way. Rich or poor, successful or unsuccessful, it's something that everyone needs help with.

## From philosophy to modern-day therapy

It was the influence of one man in the 1950s that changed things: the New York-based psychoanalyst Dr Albert Ellis. He changed tack in his clinical approach and started a major shift in the therapy world with his groundbreaking REBT – rational emotive behaviour therapy – the first form of 'cognitive therapy'.

Modern psychotherapy owes a huge debt to the ancient tradition of the Stoics. Albert Ellis's therapy, which he derived from this philosophy, was the foundation for introducing the world to this new way of thinking.

It paved the way for a revolution resulting in a worldwide acceptance of different forms of 'cognitive therapy', most famously (and perhaps most effective) a form of evidence-based treatment called cognitive behaviour therapy (CBT), which has changed the lives of millions of people around the world.

After studying Epictetus' ideas, he emphasised that as humans our disturbance about an 'adversity' results from both the adversity we are experiencing and also what we tell ourselves about it. If it was just the event or adversity, then everybody who experienced this would feel and act in the same way. He made us aware of how humans construct their own differing realities.

He defined these situations as negative events that trigger negative feelings in us, causing us discomfort and setting off a process of 'distorted thinking'. So it is up to us to take control of how we interpret and deal with situations.

His emphasis was to teach people that it is impossible to change the past – rejecting all of Freud's teachings – but we can change how we think, feel and behave *today*.

## Take back control

As we discussed earlier, control was the key message from the Stoics. They spent most of their time observing human psychology. They were trying to spread the message that we should acknowledge that all emotions come from within – it is what we tell ourselves that creates our feelings. So we are able to take control of how we interpret and deal with situations.

They recognised the fundamental point that what is under our control – our thoughts – are the source of our suffering, meaning we can, to some degree, control our suffering.

So, what is in our control and what is not? Epictetus reminds us:

*Things in our control are opinion, pursuit, desire, aversion, and, in a word, whatever are our own actions. Things not in our control are body, property, reputation, command and, in one word, whatever are not our own actions.*

ENCHIRIDION EPICTETUS (*C.* AD 125)

So we should be equipped to deal with this in a healthy manner if things don't go our way. The Stoics were aware of what we would now call stress management, and how much of our stress and anxiety is self-imposed. Their message was simple: we have to change ourselves rather than engaging in a futile attempt to change the world around us. There are consequences of pursuing those things not in our direct control. *We* need to change – in other words to be aware of things that are not up to us and mentally prepare for this to avoid dissatisfaction in daily life.

Seneca, for example, had strong opinions on changing our viewpoints – our stories – so that our life is more aligned to our goals and aspirations. If we let the opinions of other people and society as a whole dictate what we feel we're capable of, we live our life without taking the risks we've always dreamed of. He felt that the responsibility for ageing well rests with the individual and that, as time is finite, you should do those things that you want to do while you still can.

He liked to point out that we squander time as we don't pay sufficient consideration to its value, because it is 'invisible', and then come to regret it. He wrote a collection of essays addressing this problem, *De Brevitate Vitae* (*On the Shortness of Life*).

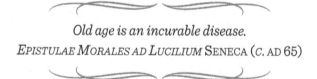

*Old age is an incurable disease.*
EPISTULAE MORALES AD LUCILIUM SENECA (C. AD 65)

This reminds me of a concert in 2019, 'Here We Go Again', at the O2 Arena in London. With a twenty-thousand capacity crowd, singer and actress Cher 'turned back time' on her sixty-year career, after conquering her fears and doubts about touring again. She had given a 'final' farewell to her fans fifteen years ago. 'I can still fit into all my old costumes,' she informed the audience.

She hadn't lost any of her sense of humour as she continued: 'I don't like it at all. Everybody claps when I tell my age and I wonder if it's 'cos I'm still alive, or I still can get into my costume?'

She ended the opening monologue with a great line: 'I have one more thing to say before I start my extravaganza: I'm seventy-three. What's your granny doing tonight?!'

## What's in our control?

The Stoics state that in certain situations when we're pursuing things that are not in our direct control, we may have luck on our side and succeed in getting this thing, or state of affairs, that we desire. All well and good.

Is there a cost attached to this? According to the Stoics there is. All the time we're wanting this thing that is 'not up to us', we're experiencing uncomfortable feelings of anxiety. This is because we're experiencing the worry of the possibility that we won't get it.

Therefore our tranquillity will be disturbed, even if we end up getting what we desire. According to the philosophers, there's a consequence for both scenarios, neither of which are good for our mental health:

- If we *don't* achieve our aim then we suffer with upset and disappointment.

> *If we pursue those things that are not up to us, then if we fail we will feel thwarted, miserable and upset, and will blame both gods and men.*
> ENCHIRIDION EPICTETUS (C. AD 125)

- Equally, if we *do* get what we want then we can't prevent suffering with anxiety in the process of attaining it.

A 'no-win' situation, as we might say in modern times.

What are the things that Epictetus felt were in our control? He was a man who said that we should be striving for 'freedom, tranquillity and calm'. He felt that we have to change ourselves rather than trying to attempt to change the world around us. We need to change our desires for things that are not up to us in order to minimise our dissatisfaction of daily life – and also the disappointment if things don't turn out well .

*You will become invincible: if you refuse to enter contests that you are capable of losing, you will never lose a contest.*
*ENCHIRIDION* EPICTETUS (*C*. AD 125)

What about those things that are up to us over which we do have complete control? He states we have complete control over our opinions, impulses, desires and aversions. When we are mentally healthy, we can form positive relationships, accept life's cards, cope with day-to-day challenges and use our abilities to reach our potential.

The key to attaining this lies predominantly in our 'thinking style'. We all engage in dysfunctional or irrational patterns of thinking. As we'll discuss later on in the next session, there are common ones that have been identified by cognitive psychotherapists.

The Stoics were ahead of their time as modern-day researchers into stress and anxiety have observed that the mental element of control (or the lack of it) is fundamental in contributing to stressful situations.

They recognised that we don't have complete control over external circumstances – our reputations, our circumstances, our day-to-day 'adversities' or the way people treat us, for example.

They believed we should direct our energy into those things that we can control. If you develop an acceptance of what's happening in life instead of demanding that things should be different, you spend less of your precious time engaging in angst and feeling frustrated. We all make plans but, as we know, life will often get in the way.

Of course, there is the human tendency to want more material things and strive each time for something bigger and shinier and better. Until the next thing comes along. For the Stoics, not needing wealth was more valuable than wealth itself. It was a change of mindset.

*The man who adapts himself to his slender means, and makes himself wealthy on a little sum, is the truly rich man.*
*LETTERS FROM A STOIC SENECA (C. AD 65)*

Wanting a less stressful life is not a bad thing. For example, staying longer in a job than you really want to, working longer hours or increasing your business revenue by making a further financial investment is not something that everybody is able or prepared to do.

There are always trade-offs in your life, and that may not align with your own personal values. You may find that another way of looking at things provides you with the same fulfilment or feeling – and at much less personal cost.

## COFFEE BREAK

An investment banker was on holiday on one of the Greek islands. A small boat was approaching and the fisherman got out and gathered several fish. The banker asked how long he was out there to catch the fish.

The fisherman replied, 'Oh, just a short while.'

The banker enquired as to why he didn't stay out longer and catch more fish.

The fisherman said it was more than enough for his family's requirements today.

The banker then asked, 'How do you spend the rest of your time?'

The fisherman replied, 'I tend to sleep late, then I fish a little, then I play with the children, take a nap, then in the evening my wife and I go over to a taverna in the village where we have a few drinks. My life is full and busy.'

The banker shook his head. 'I spend my time advising clients how to make things bigger and better,' he said. 'If you were to spend more time out there fishing, you would be able to sell the fish and then eventually buy a bigger boat. Your catch from the bigger boat would then enable you to eventually buy several boats and then in no time you would have a fleet. With that quantity of catch you could sell the fish directly to a processor and then in time have your own cannery.

'You'd have to leave the island and move to a metropolis of course.'

The fisherman said: 'Leave the island? How long would all this take?'

The banker replied: 'Maybe ten years or so, all being well.'

'*Ten years?!* What then?' the fisherman replied.

'Here's the best bit,' the banker said, 'when the time is right you can float on the stock market and you could make millions.'

'Millions – what then?'

The banker replied: '*What then?* A carefree life. You could retire, move to a small island and every day you could sleep late, fish a little, play with the kids, take a nap, go over to a taverna in the village with your wife in the evenings for a few drinks.'

# It's as Easy as ABC

## From ancient philosophy to modern psychology

*The best years of your life are the ones in which you decide your problems are your own. You do not blame them on your mother, the ecology, or the president. You realise that you control your own destiny.*

ALBERT ELLIS

Nobody – not even Freud – has had a greater impact in the field of psychotherapy than Albert Ellis. In addition to winning numerous research awards, in 2003 he was voted by the American Psychological Association as the second most influential psychologist in history, just behind Carl Rogers (Freud came in at third). His approach has helped improve the lives of millions of people.

In 1955 he created a more down-to-earth form of therapy that focused not on the past but the present. His rational emotive behaviour therapy (REBT) provided concepts that immediately seeped into cognitive psychology, psychotherapy and other areas of mainstream psychology.

His contribution caused a major shift in the 'tectonic plates' of psychotherapy. He was critical of the Freudian technique as he declared:

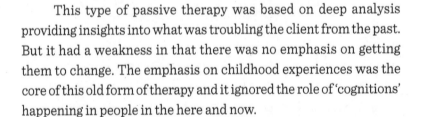

*Freudian therapists do a lot of listening and very little persuading.*
PSYCHOLOGY TODAY ALBERT ELLIS (JANUARY 2001)

This type of passive therapy was based on deep analysis providing insights into what was troubling the client from the past. But it had a weakness in that there was no emphasis on getting them to change. The emphasis on childhood experiences was the core of this old form of therapy and it ignored the role of 'cognitions' happening in people in the here and now.

Conversely, Ellis's methods were based on helping people to understand that we can't change the past but we can change how we think and therefore feel and behave today. It is the problems we are facing *now*, rather than in the past, which are important. Our 'suffering' is happening in the present. The 'cards' we are dealt that cause us problems and stress are being dealt right now.

## You feel the way you think

Ellis could see that most people were not living a good life and spent much of the time with some sort of psychological distress. He would show his clients that it was their philosophies of life that led to their sorrows. By accepting that life, for everybody, will always come with a certain amount of suffering, people could improve their lives without medication. The key to it, he showed, was thinking in a healthy way – a different way. He said, 'You mainly feel the way you think.'

There are helpful and unhelpful ways of looking at any situation or problem that we encounter. His message in his consulting room and lectures and workshops was simple. It is what we tell ourselves that creates our feelings. The key is to modify and question those unhelpful thought patterns that lead to negative emotions. We have the power to think – *and to think about our thinking.*

After practising psychotherapy and becoming less and less enamoured by the results in his consulting room, Ellis went back to reading the ancient philosophy of Epictetus. This Stoic philosopher was pivotal to the spread of Stoicism and inspired Ellis to raise awareness of the fact that we disturb ourselves by the way we choose to look at things.

As we discussed in Session 3, Stoicism is a philosophy that, more than two thousand years later, still fits in well with our twenty-first-century lives as we grapple with those perennial concerns about the life we are born into. How should we live that life? How do we deal with all those problems and setbacks that life throws at us?

Answering those questions is a tall order, but the Stoics devised a kind of 'personal operating system' for daily life, with a set of ethical values that everybody could be steered by in order to live a good life, despite the inevitable uncertainty and stress that we all suffer.

Noting that life in modern society still had parallels with ancient times, Ellis demonstrated that it is not circumstances and people that *make* us feel and behave the way we do. It is our beliefs, our attitudes towards a situation – in other words our *thinking*.

These philosophical principles, combined with an awareness and internalisation of the 'ABC' model, which was devised by Ellis and can be used in daily living, can promote good mental health and completely change your life. He introduced us to REBT, the first 'cognitive therapy', which was both a treatment *and* a philosophy.

## The birth of cognitive behavioural therapies

Albert Ellis's principles were to become a major therapeutic tool that influenced the beginning of the 'cognitive model' of psychotherapy. This led to the subsequent development of the widely known and practised cognitive behavioural therapy (CBT) that was created by Aaron Beck in the 1960s.

These therapies are now the principal treatments used by mental health practitioners around the world for treating a number of different psychological conditions.

At the core of Ellis's framework was his ABC model of emotional disturbance which showed that we all have the capacity to create our own negative or positive emotions. It is our beliefs that determine our emotional and behavioural responses to events or situations in life.

He showed how every life situation begins with an **'A'** which refers to a situation, the 'activator' or 'activating event', or what some practitioners later termed 'adversity'. It's the circumstance that happens *before* we feel ourselves experiencing an emotion. Imagine you're trying to further your professional career by gaining a qualification, and you fail one of the exam subjects. The activating event is that you've failed one of your papers.

Your **'B'** then represents your 'belief' about the situation (your thoughts). This is our *interpretation* of it, the story we tell ourselves. You may believe that you're not cut out to pursue a further qualification and this represents your thinking process.

This leads to the **'C'**, the consequences, which are both emotional *and* behavioural. How we feel and then react. You may feel despondent and then tell your manager that you've decided not to continue with the course, thereby reducing your chances of career progression.

Ellis wanted to illustrate, in common with the ancient philosophy that had inspired him, that it is not the A that causes the C, it is the B. So he devised his model to illustrate how beliefs are the cause of emotional and behavioural responses. This was derived from his strong attachment to Epictetus' famous quote:

*Men are disturbed not by things but by the view which they take of them...*
ENCHIRIDION EPICTETUS (C. AD 125)

## Irrational beliefs

The ABC method was a straightforward and memorable way for Ellis's clients to understand the 'activators' to their emotions and their subsequent behaviours. It provided a clear framework for breaking down the mind's internal process into constituent parts: how beliefs (and not the activating events) are the cause of our emotional and behavioural responses.

The crux of the model is that we instinctively blame the situation (A) for the consequences (C), whereas in fact it is our beliefs (B) that are to blame. Furthermore, those beliefs can be irrational which can make us feel sad, angry, anxious or depressed, which then lead to behaviours that are counter-productive.

So the aim of his REBT was to help people analyse and then

### The A-B-C Model:

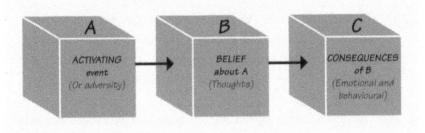

change their irrational thinking to a more reasonable and rational way in each situation.

Ellis's influence was groundbreaking in the worlds of psychology and psychotherapy. Modern research confirms those ancient truths. No practitioner before him had introduced the connection between how people in their everyday lives were mainly responsible for their own negative feelings and distress. All of this because of their beliefs (or thoughts) about a particular experience.

He wanted to bring awareness of the fact that we disturb ourselves by the way we choose to look at things. He had formulated a theoretical and philosophical model of his therapy and then proved the scientific benefits of adopting this form of treatment.

He demonstrated how many of our emotional and behavioural problems derive from our own unrealistic and distorted beliefs about the situations we encounter, and also how we feel we should be treated by others. Looking at our everyday life in modern times he revisited the ancient belief that it is not situations and people that ultimately make us feel and react the way we do. *It's the way we think about the situation that is responsible.*

Take this situation, for example. You've been persuaded to enrol on a group singing class.

- **Thoughts (your beliefs)** I don't believe my voice is as good as the others in the group.

- **Emotions (how you feel)** I feel anxious and humiliated.

- **Behaviour (how you behave/act in the situation)** I'll sit at the back of the room away from the teacher so I can't be heard.

Your thinking in this situation influences the emotions you are feeling and how you behave. It's important to remember that your thoughts, feelings and behaviour also influence each other in an interdependent fashion. Your feelings (derived from your thoughts) also influence your thinking, which sets off a cycle of reinforcement.

There are helpful or unhelpful ways of how we can look at any situation or problem that we encounter. By being flexible in our thoughts, our attitude when faced with negative situations could be altered to more 'healthy' negative feelings like concern, sorrow, disappointment and/or productive anger.

It's important to realise that negative thoughts that result in negative emotions are not the problem for us in everyday living. Difficulties arise when they prevent you from taking active steps to *alter* the circumstances for the better or hanging on to those feelings when the thing that you're facing is something you cannot control, which then causes you distress.

When we become disturbed by an adversity, it's what we tell ourselves about that adversity that decides how we feel, according to Ellis. (We spoke about the stories we tell ourselves in Session 1, you'll remember.) If it was just the adverse situation that caused us a disturbance then everybody who went through that same situation would feel and behave the same. We all have our own subjective view of what we would regard as an adversity.

I remember reading about a writer, James Agee, who came

into contact with an elderly lady in the USA during the era of the Great Depression. She lived in a tiny shack with dirt floors, no heat or indoor plumbing. Agee asked her, 'If someone came and offered you money to help you out, what would you do?' The lady waited for a while before answering, 'I guess I'd give it to the poor.'

So your thinking is responsible for your feelings and your subsequent behaviour. Your feelings affect your thinking and behaviour, and your behaviour affects your thinking and your feelings. This creates a vicious circle, which needs to be broken.

When we encounter failure in any area we experience feelings like regret, annoyance and sorrow. These are all healthy negative feelings. Indeed, we couldn't exist without these feelings.

Ellis acknowledged that it is impossible to completely rid ourselves of irrational thinking (more about that in Session 5) but that our lives can change immeasurably if we reduce their *frequency, intensity* and *duration.*

At the core of his groundbreaking REBT was the formulation of his ABC model, which we discussed earlier. This powerful technique can be applied as a kind of daily 'personal operating system' to guide us through life. It makes us aware of our thoughts in the moment. It's almost like 'alchemy'. You're probably familiar with this term when it refers to turning a less valuable substance into one that is more valuable. Lead into gold was the common description.

Well, we demonstrate a kind of alchemy when we transform our consciousness by altering our thoughts and beliefs so that it changes our inner state, which then changes our outlook – and subsequent behaviour. Then 'magic happens'.

## Demands or 'preferences?

We have this magical capacity to reframe our thoughts, which changes our feelings – and then the circumstances – all through words.

Ellis acknowledged that we tend to attribute things that happen to us – or the way that people behave towards us – as being responsible for the way we *feel*. Therefore if we feel angry, anxious, depressed, frustrated or whatever, we mistakenly assume it's because of other people or circumstances. The key to living a good life was an acceptance of *reality* – good or bad. Only then could we become emotionally healthy. This required acceptance and it had to come in three areas:

**Unconditional self-acceptance** People should forgive themselves for not being perfect. They should continue to make mistakes and believe at the same time that they are still worthwhile. We have to accept ourselves and recognise that we all have flaws as well as having good points.

**Unconditional other-acceptance** Accept that people won't always treat us fairly. There is no reason why they should treat us fairly.

**Unconditional life-acceptance** Accept that life will not play out as we would like. There is no reason why it should, and although we may experience unpleasant situations it is bearable.

Ellis stressed that we should pay particular attention and make ourselves aware of the distinction between 'appropriate' or 'inappropriate' emotions. We can't get rid of all those negative emotions like feeling sad, regretful, annoyed or disappointed. These are healthy responses that in some instances may be appropriate to the events and situations we encounter.

So if we acknowledge that – whether we like it or not – life is not fair, then we change our emotions. As children we were commonly used to complaining 'that's not fair' – when we were consigned to the bedroom, forbidden to have our laptop around the dinner table, had to clear up before being allowed to watch TV. As adults this phrase takes on a new meaning as we deal with life's daily vicissitudes and we rail against the universe and realise that indeed, life is often not fair.

It brings to mind American late-night television host Johnny Carson's observation: 'Life's not fair. If life was fair, Elvis would still be alive and all the impersonators would be dead.'

We spend time *demanding* that things should be a certain way in life or that they should turn out this way or that way ('demandingness' as Ellis called it). The inflexibility of our beliefs is the main problem in causing us upset in life, he argued. If we could change our thinking to regard them as *preferences*, our world would change.

How much better is it to 'prefer' that the train will be on time today; that the boss is in a sunnier mood than yesterday; that the team will like your written proposal on office change; that the parcel arrives in the morning rather than the afternoon.

Our beliefs influence our thoughts; our *thoughts* influence the way that we *feel* and *behave*. Our beliefs are our unconscious assumptions that guide our thoughts.

We all have those deep beliefs that are an amalgam of our past and current experiences that expose themselves in our self-talk. They inevitably wield great power over the way that we 'frame' situations.

## Thinking, emotions and behaviour

In his Friday Night workshop sessions, Ellis found that most people were unaware of this connection between our thinking, our emotions and how we consequently behave. He would demonstrate how events that occurred did not lead to the same response in *everyone*. It was the belief or attitude of the individual that led to a particular feeling or emotion and how they viewed the situation.

Later on, as the awareness and popularity of his ABC model

## Disputing the A-B-C Model:

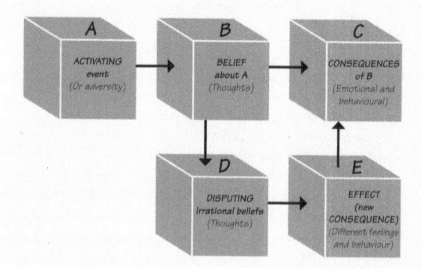

grew, Ellis added a two-step suffix for clarity. He called it the ABCDE model (see opposite). Here the aim was to show how 'disputing' (D) the original belief in favour of a more rational and healthier one leads to a new 'effect' (E).

According to Ellis, when we have irrational beliefs we tend to ignore the positive, exaggerate the negative, distort reality and over-generalise. So the person who has multiple irrational beliefs will go through life distorting reality, at the mercy of repeated negative feelings and emotional pain, being self-critical and suffering from anxiety. By contrast the person who has, or cultivates, a more rational way of thinking can see things as they really are and handle challenges more successfully.

The ABC model, with its 'cause and effect' sequence, highlights our dysfunctional thoughts and attitudes. It shows how the feelings we experience and our behaviour are determined by our 'cognitive' interpretation of the event.

In other words the way a person perceives a situation is more a function of their *reaction* than the situation itself. In most instances as we encounter situations this internal experience happens so quickly we're unaware of our conscious thinking process. The idea of Ellis's ABC model was to help a person *recognise* and then *dispute* those irrational beliefs and accept the rational beliefs.

It enables you to examine the 'cause and effect' of your own reactions and identify your dysfunctional attitudes (thoughts and beliefs). How we feel and behave (the C – consequences) is not determined by the event or circumstance (the A – activator) but by our cognitive interpretation of the situation, in other words the B. Then, when appropriate, you can gain back control by disputing your thoughts. It was as easy as ABC!

Can you think back to something that happened recently that sticks in your mind because you wish you 'could have played it differently' because of your strong reaction?

What was the A? How did it progress to the C? Now, perhaps more importantly, what was the B that took you there? (In other words, what came *before* you experienced the feelings that caused the C?)

The crux of Ellis's REBT was that it is the thought, in other words the belief (B), not the (A), the activating event, that causes the feelings and consequences (C) in any situation.

Let's take an example:

The **(A)**: *My friend is late meeting me again.*

The **(B)**: *She's always late. It's not as though we don't make arrangements well in advance.*

These are the beliefs, the stories we tell ourselves, about situations that we discussed earlier. These are responsible for our thoughts.

We assign subjective meanings, you'll remember, about

events as they occur. We all have 'irrational beliefs' from time to time that occur from a faulty thinking process that is not backed up by evidence.

The **(C)**: *I feel frustrated, angry, disrespected, disappointed. I decide to be 'unavailable' on further occasions as I don't want to experience these uncomfortable emotions. I let my friend know I'm busy for the foreseeable future.*

The 'C' refers to the consequences of the situation – your emotional and behavioural response.

**If you think of examples of your own, you can break down much of your behaviour in day-to-day life into an ABC situation.** Doing so forces you to analyse your thinking process and can spare you much angst and unnecessary anxiety.

In many cases our irrational thinking precludes us from trying to find a solution; we just accept our thoughts without 'disputing' them to check whether they are realistic.

After you've disputed your possible irrational thinking, you start to develop an alternative thought process which leads to different beliefs.

In the previous example, the situation has resulted in no more contact between the two friends. Now, with a change of thinking after rational analysis and deciding to 'dispute' the thinking, we can look at the D and E of the model.

The **(D)**: *Well, she's not always late. It's just that she has been three of the last five times we've met. She apologises, but doesn't give me a reason. That would help a bit. But at least she does apologise, I suppose. She might have a reason that she hasn't told me about.*

Disputing your thoughts and beliefs allows you to gain more self-awareness of your thinking and avoid jumping to conclusions (which is a common thinking error, as we'll see later). It could even help point you towards a solution.

The **(E)**: *Maybe there's a problem and she doesn't feel able to tell me about it. I'll ask her.*

The 'effects' happen after you've done your disputation of your possible irrational thinking. You start to develop an alternative thought process which leads to different beliefs.

Let's say the person in our previous example decides to ask her friend why she was late. She may find that there was a problem. Her friend's flatmate – who normally gives her a lift to the station – gets back from work a few minutes late sometimes, so she ends up getting a later train.

Her personality was such that she felt embarrassed about ringing to say she'd be a little late and thought it was OK, as she felt her friend was 'easy going'. When they discussed this, they agreed that in future her friend should just text or call to say what was happening.

So much of our irrational thinking errors derive from our beliefs, which of course drive our thinking and behaviour. Obviously, sometimes our emotions – such as anger, frustration, fear, and regret – are perfectly *healthy* responses and are appropriate to the (A) when we analyse them. If we apply the ABC model, it will confirm that the emotions are *appropriate*.

**It's when the emotional reactions are a result of *irrational* beliefs and therefore cause unnecessary conflict and suffering that following it through to the full ABCDE is helpful.**

Let's look at some situations where the ABC model can be applied.

## SCENARIO 1

**The activating event (A)** Lauren is at the theatre with her husband. During the interval in the bar area, she sees the lady who sometimes babysits their children coming towards them.

'Look, that's Sue,' she says to her husband. To her surprise, Sue walks straight past them both without saying a word or even acknowledging their presence.

**Lauren's beliefs and thoughts (B)** Lauren thinks, 'I can't believe she didn't say hello. What did I do to possibly upset her? Last month when she was at the house, I know we came back twenty minutes late because the taxi was delayed picking us up, but she assured us she didn't mind. I did pay her quite a lot for the extra time. That's so rude. I helped her out last time when she needed to borrow a steam cleaner . . . I was going to call her in a couple of weeks' time to book her for that reunion evening. I'll get somebody else now. Sarah uses a reliable babysitter. I'll ask her for the phone number . . .'

**The behavioural and emotional consequences of her thoughts (C)** Lauren had bad feelings and couldn't concentrate during the second half of Les Miserables (which describes exactly how she felt!).

When she got home that evening, feeling upset, she said to her bemused mother, who had been babysitting, 'I'm not using Sue again.'

Lauren doesn't call Sue the next time. She gets the name and details of an alternative babysitter.

Put simply, how Lauren thought about this incident affected how she felt and dictated her subsequent behaviour.

Now, how about the 'reality' of the event, which she discovers when she doesn't jump to conclusions?

## SCENARIO 2 (MORE RATIONAL WAY OF THINKING)

**The activating event (A)** 'Look, that's Sue,' Lauren says to her husband. To her surprise, Sue walks straight past them both without saying a word or even acknowledging their presence.

**Lauren's beliefs and thoughts (B)** Lauren thinks, 'I don't think she saw us. She looks really worried – did you see the expression on her face? I'll never get to her, she's dashed through that crowd now. I'll give her a call tomorrow to make sure she's OK. I was going to call her soon anyway to fix up an evening for her to come round.'

**The behavioural and emotional consequences of her thoughts (C)** Lauren calls Sue the next day: 'Hello, Sue. Are you OK? Guess what. We saw you at *Les Miserables* last night, you were dashing through the bar area.'

'Oh, Lauren, I'm sorry I didn't see you. It's not surprising though; I had a bit of a mini-disaster. I was crying so much after that scene with Valjean when he rescues Cosette, and one of my disposable contact lenses fell out. I was rushing to the cloakroom trying to beat the crowds, to put another one in. Luckily, I carry spares in my handbag. Anyway, how did you enjoy the show? It was my third time!'

Two different results after thinking about the event differently.

## REFRAMING YOUR THOUGHTS

Well, isn't this the kind of thing that happens all the time in life? It illustrates the thoughts-feelings-action process that occurs when we are in a given situation. In this example, Lauren's thinking affected how she felt and what she did – the actions she decided to take.

We can look at circumstances and situations, and by 'reframing' the event we change the outcome of a situation with our subsequent behaviour.

In Scenario 1, Lauren felt upset and her subsequent behaviour resulted in the loss of a babysitter as she'd decided to look for a new one. All of this made her feel even worse. She'd taken a view or interpretation of a situation, as we all do from time to time, without much evidence to support it.

The alternate way of thinking in Scenario 2, where she changed her thoughts or beliefs from being 'snubbed' to being 'concerned' for Sue, meant that her *feelings* were different – she wasn't upset – and her behaviour was different – she got in touch with Sue the next day. Changing your thinking results in changing your emotional reaction to situations.

Our thoughts and feelings are responsible for our behaviour. So that means we can take control of situations by thinking in healthy ways.

By doing this Lauren was at least able to correct any misunderstandings that may have arisen on both sides. In this case, the reasons were quite innocent.

How many times do we engage in this sort of mind-reading or jump to conclusions?

## The 'alchemy' of disputing our thoughts

We're all at the mercy of the slings and arrows of daily life, but the ABC model highlights how we do have control over how we interpret and therefore think about a situation. One way of thinking, based on our irrational belief, may immobilise us. After challenging or disputing this with an alternative belief that is less irrational, we may be able to change our behaviour for a more favourable outcome.

Ellis's ABC model is a powerful technique that we can all apply as a kind of 'personal operating system' to guide us through life. It makes us aware of our thoughts in the moment.

We have this magical capacity to 'reframe' our thoughts, which changes our feelings – and then our circumstances – all through words.

*You have been formed of three parts – body, breath and mind. Of these, the first two are yours insofar as they are only in your care. The third alone is truly yours.*
*MEDITATIONS* MARCUS AURELIUS (*C.* AD 171–5)

It's worth repeating the important premise that forms the cornerstone of much of what we've discussed. Just because we think something, that doesn't mean it's true. Get used to accepting that some things are just thoughts rather than facts.

When we engage in rational thinking we objectively see things as they really are. If our thinking is irrational then we distort reality by misrepresenting things that happen.

## COFFEE BREAK

A man was concerned that his wife's hearing was not as good as it used to be. She was not answering his questions. He kept repeating himself and the whole thing was causing him frustration every day.

He called their doctor and asked for his advice.

'Try this,' the doctor said. 'We need to gauge the severity of her hearing problem. Stand about 40 feet away from her, and in a normal conversational speaking tone, see if she hears you. If not go to 30 feet. Then 20 feet. Then 10 feet.

'So that's four attempts you should try. After that carry on until you get a response from her.'

That evening the man's wife is in the kitchen cooking dinner. From about 40 feet away in a normal voice he asks, 'Honey, what's for dinner?'

No response. He moves closer to the kitchen, about 30 feet away from her. 'Dolly, what's for dinner?'

Again, he gets no response. Then 20 feet away. No response.

Then he walks up to the kitchen door, about 10 feet away. She's standing to the side chopping vegetables. 'What's for dinner tonight?'

Yet again, there is no response from her. So he walks right up to her. 'Dolly, what's for dinner?'

She looks up at him and in an exasperated tone says: 'For goodness sake, for the FIFTH time, steak and kidney pudding!'

# Worry and Anxiety

## The power of irrational thinking

*My life has been full of terrible misfortunes, most of which never happened...*
*Essais* Michel de Montaigne (1595)

Part of the human condition is to engage in feelings of stress, regret, anxiety, fear – the list goes on. We time travel to the past to be reminded of negative experiences and regrets about what we should (or shouldn't) have done. Then we'll move on to that unknown land of the future and engage in some Grade A anxiety. It causes our thoughts to race with fear and worry.

Apprehension over the unknown affects our emotional and physical health as it follows through with the mind–body connection. We all suffer from anxiety at some time or another. It is our emotional response to worry.

We worry about:

• Actual or real problems that we have to cope with; and

• Problems that could occur in the future.

Feelings of anxiety emanate from our fear of an imagined future rather than some uncomfortable feeling or situation we're experiencing in the present.

What you're also aware of by now is the importance of the subjective meaning that we give to our thoughts and feelings. As we know, these internal experiences are responsible for producing our emotions of worry and anxiety.

It's all down to how we're interpreting and judging events based on the thoughts that are running through our mind. We need to consider each of those anxiety-inducing thoughts individually. Has it ever happened before? Why should it happen now? Is the worry realistic?

## State and trait anxiety

We're never really in control of our lives the way we like to imagine that we are. Some people are predisposed to having an anxious nature and will always feel the need to try and put themselves in the position of being in charge over circumstances. We have to take back control by examining our thinking and disputing the beliefs and attitudes that are responsible for our thoughts.

To do so, we must first distinguish between two types of anxiety, which help us to analyse our own thinking and how we can challenge our thoughts to minimise mental anguish.

We anticipate threats about things that may *possibly* occur in the future. This is called **'state anxiety'**: the feeling that something dreadful may happen. It's something that all of us experience and is characterised by the fact that these threats cease to be a worry after the situation or event has passed.

> 'They're warning us about Storm Munch approaching in the next few days. Does that mean no flights? How will I get to the wedding?'

> 'I'll have to ask Tom and Hilary to come in for a meeting next month and break it to them that we'll have to cut their hours.'

> 'What will they find in the car service? The gearbox didn't sound too healthy. How much could that cost me?'

Much more troubling are those of us who seem to be in a *permanent* state of anxiety: a situation we term **'trait anxiety'**. From childhood we all develop specific ways of interpreting events and looking at the world. Sometimes experiences from early life can lead to a personality or disposition that tends towards expecting the worst and a reduced sense of self-esteem. An outlook that sees on the horizon all the things that could go wrong. The thing to remember is that anxiety triggers our flight-or-flight stress response.

## Words can wound and words can heal

We sometimes hear the phrase 'anxious children equals anxious adults'. It's also easy to see how children may internalise their parents' own anxieties based on their view of the outside world. It's been suggested that some parents who have a 'perfectionist' attitude, or who spend a lot of time being excessively critical of their children and their behaviour, may instill these attitudes in them from an early age.

For example, emotionally charged words from others, both in childhood and later on in life, can affect a person's confidence. You might remember the childhood rhyme: 'Sticks and stones may break my bones, but words will never hurt me.' But is this true? Words can wound and words can heal.

It's human nature that we don't tend to forget hurtful words. Sometimes just an innocent turn of phrase can do lifelong damage to a person's psyche and self-esteem. As most people will attest, long after physical injuries have healed and faded from memory over the years, it's hurtful words that we remember.

## The anxiety spiral

The situation is invariably made worse for many people who unconsciously believe that if we worry enough, it can *prevent* something awful happening.

You can understand that if the situation results in nothing awful happening, it reinforces the belief that worrying about it did actually help. So, as that worry habit persists and as those negative 'hands of cards' are dealt and pile up, it can tip over into extreme anxiety.

When we're experiencing worry and anxiety, we may be sad and miserable, and all this angst serves to deprive us of a state of relative happiness. We may find it difficult to concentrate, and as the anxiety increases you may feel hopeless, overwhelmed and guilty. Then your self-esteem goes. You may cut down on your interactions with people and withdraw from other activities.

Our propensity for engaging in various forms of irrational thinking may keep us stuck in the anxiety spiral. There is something else to contend with. There is an 'opposite' to this: anxiety also *influences* the way we think.

We all experience mood changes that are transient and fluctuate up and down in response to various stressors, and they are usually short-lived. But when worry and fear occupies too much of a person's life – because of its intensity and frequency – these anxious feelings can become overwhelming and can push a person into a deeper and deeper state of depression.

The negative influence that anxiety has on the way we think may show itself in our tendency to be more self-critical and attribute self-blame as we dredge up past behaviour and experiences.

Your memory becomes selective, leaning towards remembering things that you may have been guilty of, bad things that have happened to you and mistakes you've made in the past. But if we didn't make mistakes, we would never learn anything in life. If you think about it, no matter what you do, *you might be making a mistake*. We don't set out on a course of action in order to ensure we make a mistake.

It's how you recover from the events and the acceptance that it doesn't define you as a person that's important. We all beat ourselves up because of this basic universal human frailty. You are not your mistake.

## What's the worst that could happen?

It's been frequently cited in surveys that between 80 and 90 per cent of our fears and worries never actually see the light of day. You may remember that oft-quoted statement attributed to Mark Twain: 'I have known many troubles in my life – and some of them actually happened.'

'Maybe that fund was not a good investment choice.'

Then the spiral starts its *downward* trajectory:

'I shouldn't have listened to John. What does he know? He can't even get the monthly budgets in on time. If the North American stocks tumble it'll take ages to recover. I can't afford to lose money on that fund, it's supposed to provide an income. And what if I were to lose my job. If the job goes then my pension fund goes. Sarah will never forgive me. She'll have to go back to full-time work. The train services are bad enough already for her. What if those regular strikes by the drivers continue. What about that extension we'd planned? How will Natasha get her own room now? I'm always promising her things without thinking clearly. She'll mope and spend even more time online. I can just imagine the conversation when I tell her.'

And so the BBC Radio *Play for Today* continues . . .

All of our mental energy is spent focusing on the worry itself rather than on solving a problem in the here and now. Even worse, it's about something that may never happen. We engage in all those 'what ifs?' that create a spiral of increasing anxiety. Is it any wonder, when we consider that most of us spend our time thinking and making plans for the future – the next five *minutes*, the next five *hours*, the next five *days*, the next five *months,* the next five *years*?

Fortunately help is at hand. We can use rational thinking for these anxiety-inducing 'what if?' thoughts by considering some useful questions that I call '*what is?* statements'.

Instead of occupying your mind with something that may never happen, consider:

1.  **What is the likelihood, on a scale of 1 to 10, that the things I am worrying about *will* happen?**

'If the economy takes a dive, they might decide to close this office. No, when I think of it, they've always said they need this as a vital hub.'

**2. What is most *likely* to happen?**

'At worst, I imagine they might reduce our hours. Maybe introduce a bit of flexi-working – from home part of the time.'

**3. What is the *best* thing that could happen?**

'They've got those proposals for those huge ten-year management contracts out for tender. If just one of those comes off, things will probably be fine.'

**4. What is the *worst* that could happen? And could I handle it if it does happen?**

'If things don't work out well, they'll no doubt give us options and also a lot of time if there any redundancies or whatever. Maybe that would be the push I need to find something else. Also, Richard's still working and about to get promoted, so no reason to worry really...'

This final one, imagining the 'worst' that could happen, was an important consideration in Stoic philosophy. Remember the 'premeditation of adversity' (*praemeditatio malorium*) from Seneca that we discussed at the end of Session 3? This was his powerful tool of mental imagery, whereby visualising setbacks or misfortunes helps us prepare for dealing with them by devising coping strategies well in advance. He also wisely advises that we take:

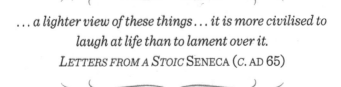

*... a lighter view of these things ... it is more civilised to
laugh at life than to lament over it.*
LETTERS FROM A STOIC SENECA (C. AD 65)

Healthy pessimism can steer us to consider the 'what ifs' that
plague us about the future. It can prepare us to work out how to deal
with the worst-case scenarios.

Positive thinking can go only so far. You may feel better but it
can make the mind less resilient when it comes to those 'neural
pathways'. We need to engage that thinking time with ways of
actually dealing with possible challenges and adversities.

By visualising possible situations that could occur in the
future, causing you worry and anxiety in the present, you can look
to a possible solution if things do turn out adversely. You're mentally
prepared and so you can minimise your stress.

Epictetus also tells us that by rehearsing every 'misfortune' –
in the absence of any real adversity – we can, in our imagination,
confront any future challenges well ahead of time. Consequently,
this can reduce our anxiety and prepare us for whatever life may
throw at us.

Using our ABC model we need to dispute our thoughts that
are making us feel anxious and downgrade them to a more healthy
feeling of *concern*. This change of feeling will then naturally change
our behaviour.

If we spend our time having those conversations with
ourselves about everything that could go wrong, we'll remain in an
agitated and fearful state. As the Stoics recommended, the same
time and energy we spend worrying would be better used to work
out solutions for these hypothetical situations, or, in the absence of
that, how you can minimise the discomfort.

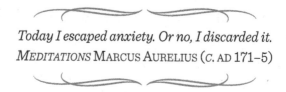

*Today I escaped anxiety. Or no, I discarded it.*
*MEDITATIONS* MARCUS AURELIUS (*C.* AD 171–5)

This was Marcus Aurelius' way of dealing with this problem of the human condition.

We spend our time being critical about who we are and what we can't do, as we apply comparisons between ourselves and other people. These thoughts often feel realistic – to us. The truth is usually different and so we have to find ways to prevent those negative statements from pulling us down.

## Focus on what you can do

We need to take the focus away from those self-critical thoughts. Focus instead on questioning those irrational thoughts about who you are and what you can do.

Psychologists have long advocated that the mind makes more association with statements that are framed within the context of 'I'. It makes your self-talk more personal and allows you to remind yourself of past achievements, strengths and talents.

So, for example:

'I managed to get on the final shortlist of three candidates for promotion on other occasions, I can do it again.'

'I know I've been told many times that I'm good at meet and greet, so I'll take that opportunity next week.'

'I managed to do this before. There's no reason it can't happen again.'

Many scientific studies have shown that engaging our mind in memories of good things that made us happy and also showing gratitude for things that we already have, has a beneficial effect on our mental health.

You may be familiar with the 'Patronus' charm if you've been in the world of J.K. Rowling's *Harry Potter*. It's a spell that the wizards could use to combat those nasty 'Dementors' that suck all good feelings from their victims.

Our real-life version of these creatures are negative feelings like anxiety, negativity, self-criticism, depression. If we can recall memories of things that inspire a feeling of gratitude, we have our own 'Patronus' charm. *Expecto Patronum.* No, that's not a phrase from the Stoics! Those are the words of the spell. Use your own affirmation (or 'spell') to banish your negative thoughts and change your feelings.

You may have seen sports players take out pieces of paper and 'cue' cards with motivating statements written on them during matches. Photographers and TV cameras often zoom in on handwritten statements that players pull out of their bags for motivation. Tennis player Serena Williams – arguably the greatest American athlete of all time – kept little affirmation 'matchbooks' which she would read during changeovers in her tennis matches. She said, 'I use positive affirmations and I try to believe in myself. Then I take things one stage at a time.'

These serve as reminders to alter your thinking in situations if you're overwhelmed by adverse feelings.

We've learned from the ABC model that we can't just tell our thoughts and feelings to go away. We have to dispute or challenge them. Expose them for what they are. You can't suppress a thought yourself. Or, even worse, when somebody obligingly tells you, 'Don't think about it.'

Daniel Wegner at Harvard University is an expert on thought suppression, and came across this sentence:

*Try to pose for yourself this task: not to think of a polar bear, and you will see that the cursed thing will come to mind every minute.*

*WINTER NOTES ON SUMMER IMPRESSIONS*
FYODOR DOSTOEVSKY (1863)

Wegner conducted a famous white polar bear experiment, to test the validity of this quote, in which participants were asked not to think of the bear. The participants were instructed to verbalise on anything for five minutes while trying not to think of a white bear.

He showed that when you're asked to do this, if you don't think of a white polar bear, what do you end up thinking? You have to think about and process each word in your mind. Eventually you get to 'polar bear', which you're being asked not to think of. His research proved that trying not to think of something caused it to 'rebound' more into the mind later on. You've actually programmed your mind to retain the words 'white polar bear'. These results eventually led to a new field of study called 'thought suppression'.

Suppose you say to your son when he borrows your brand-new car, 'Please don't scrape the tyres against the kerb.' The mind processes each word, and the subconscious focuses on 'scrape' and 'tyres'.

If you rephrase the request as, 'Please try and keep a distance from the kerb', the mind focuses on 'distance' and 'kerb', and in a less negative fashion than if you had warned him against scraping the tyres.

How about when your 'inner talk', just before your speech, has you thinking, 'I mustn't forget my lines and if I do I mustn't stutter, look flustered and sigh.' The 'rebound' has you focusing on 'forget', 'stutter', 'flustered'.

How about: 'If something slips my mind, I'll remain calm, confident and move on to the next point and maybe go back to it.'

The 'rebound' now focuses on 'calm' 'confident', 'move on'.

Later research showed that when trying *not* to think of something, a certain part of our brain avoids the thought, but at the same time another part of our brain keeps 'watch' every now and then to make sure the thought doesn't reappear. The result: it only serves to bring the thought back.

## The power of distorted or 'irrational' thinking

We all engage in distorted or 'irrational thinking'. Usually this is an inaccurate or exaggerated form of thinking with a tendency to think in terms of 'absolutes'.

Our mind is quite capable of distorting reality. After all, you're in charge – you give the orders! You ask your mind to process thoughts that don't accurately describe or predict events. But it is important to look at irrational thoughts and analyse them in order to re-evaluate them and make them match reality. We're not trying to rationalise away every bad thing that happens; just making sure they more accurately reflect reality.

Psychologists have identified the most common forms of distortion. See if you can recall the last time you exercised that type of thinking error.

### OVER-GENERALISING

This is when a negative conclusion is formed about other people, ourselves or life more generally after witnessing just one instance or piece of evidence. Over-generalising is characterised by thinking that often contains the words 'always', 'never', 'nobody', 'everyone', 'the world is ...' You come up with the idea that this is what *always* happens.

'Everybody in the check-out queue is slow.'

'Nobody will trust me again after that mistake.'

'I never win anything.'

One mistake and you're a failure. One person out of ten finds fault with the accuracy of your report – you're incompetent. You miss the slip road for the motorway – you're a terrible driver. A critical comment concerns you for a day, a week, a month or even longer.

Whether you say these things or whether they are part of your inner self-talk these are all extreme statements that lead to a perception of a situation being worse than it is in reality. They make you feel bad. At least when you're voicing this to someone they may be kind enough to dispute some of these statements. But with your self-talk there's no 'referee'.

Recall the last time you engaged in this thinking. What effect did it have?

## MIND-READING

One of most common forms of unhealthy thinking, especially when our self-esteem is low, is telepathy. We think we know what a person (or people) is thinking. That's fine for a stage performance, if you can pull it off. But in real life it's more often than not a case of jumping to conclusions.

What conclusions do we typically reach? That people are forming *negative* conclusions about us. All sorts of imaginative scenarios are played out in the mind.

'He's not going to return my call because I wasn't able to help him out last time.'

'She thinks I'm a threat, so she won't shortlist me, so I'm not going to bother applying.'

'I know he thinks I'm boring because he kept looking at his phone.'

You divine how people are feeling towards you. Yet you are jumping to conclusions with no real evidence. So, in effect, you take your *own* negative opinions about yourself (which, of course, you translate as facts) and you believe that others are in agreement with you. All deduced by telepathy.

Have you noticed that your 'gift' of telepathy doesn't extend to mind-reading *positive* thoughts relating to you!

## MAGNIFICATION AND FILTERING

You may be quite familiar with this one. You take the negative details from a situation and then magnify them – making mountains out of molehills – and conveniently and self-destructively filter out all the positive elements, which completely distorts the sequence of events.

You focus on the one bad thing about a situation. You give a successful presentation but forget the name of one contributor – awful. You look 'a million dollars' in that new skirt at your function but there's a loose thread which is plain for you to see – awful. The conference you organised goes very well, but the taxis are twenty minutes late for pick-ups at the end of the day – awful.

We magnify the 'awfulness' of a situation and minimise and screen out anything positive about it.

## ALL-OR-NOTHING (POLARISED THINKING)

All-or-nothing thinking is when we view things in extremes that are either good or bad. This extends to ourselves, others and situations. It is often termed black-or-white thinking as there are no shades of grey or any middle ground. It is unrealistic and often unhelpful because most of the time reality exists somewhere between two extremes.

This kind of thinking sets you up for total failure in many instances, with disappointment and self-criticism all taking their toll. It imposes standards that are difficult to achieve. It encourages perfectionist-type thinking. It's a very rigid form of thinking that causes much psychological stress and contributes to a lot of anxiety.

'If I can't lose seven pounds by the end of the month I'm hopeless.'

'If I don't get those exam grades, I'm not going to that party on Saturday.'

This type of irrational thinking can lower your self-esteem as it affects how you view yourself. The underlying belief is that a person's worth is determined by achievement.

## PERSONALISING

Personalising is a common type of thinking where you take the blame for things that are not necessarily your fault. You attribute what somebody says as a direct reaction to you. Passing remarks are taken as personal criticism. You end up feeling guilty over things that are not your fault, or are not directed at you.

Your partner says the lounge needs a tidy-up and he'll help you – so it's a criticism of your contribution towards housekeeping. The manager of another department at work pops in to your office and comments, 'The lighting's not very good in here, is it?' You take that as a personal criticism. A member of your baking class who's usually very talkative is a bit quiet today. You take that as a personal criticism.

People with a tendency to personalise will spend a lot of their cognitive life experiencing feelings of hurt and guilt, often unfounded. It can fracture relationships too.

## BLAMING

This is the opposite of personalising. Other people, organisations or the 'universe' are at fault and causing our problems. You are a victim of the situation or other people's thoughtlessness and meanness. Your energy is expended on casting or apportioning blame, rather than seeking a way to rectify or get over the problem.

If blame can be given over to someone or something else, then there is no need to look at your own thinking and behaviour to see whether you may have contributed – or whether your inter- pretation may be at fault. So you avoid taking personal responsibility.

'That company ruined my life.'

'They single-handedly ruined the day.'

'If he hadn't done that, I wouldn't have reacted.'

'She made me feel terrible.'

'It's because of him that I shouted at the checkout person.'

## SELF-BLAME

Here, in contrast to the previous type of thinking, you're taking responsibility for things that have happened that are *not* your fault or your responsibility.

'I shouldn't have got you those tickets for the theatre. Then you wouldn't have lost your ring up in the dress circle.'

'If only I'd chosen those other decorators, they might have done a better job.'

'Should have known not to trust the baking times for
that recipe.'

## PERFECTIONIST THINKING

Perfectionism may sound like an attractive trait, but it can make
life very stressful. High standards are to be applauded in any area
of life, but when applied to ourselves can cause problems.

Two types of perfectionism have been identified, adaptive and
maladaptive. Adaptive perfectionism is a situation whereby we can
maintain our high standards and, more importantly, have the
capacity to cope when we are unable to meet our objective.
Conversely, maladaptive attitudes result in the person suffering
major upset at their *perceived* failure.

If your perfectionist tendencies are mainly deriving from
your internal self-talk – as opposed to pressure from external
sources – then we can question and dispute our thinking and
attitudes using the ABC model.

For example, suppose you're having to deliver a report for your
department by a certain date. What are your beliefs? That it is
better to deliver *no* report rather than an imperfect (in your eyes)
one? Wouldn't your boss rather have a report that's delivered on
time, rather than no report at all? Your 'subjective' thoughts relating
to the quality of your report may not be true. Sometimes just enough
is good enough.

## FORTUNE-TELLING

This is where we engage in a touch of clairvoyancy. You know how
something's going to turn out, so you engage in avoidance and don't
put yourself in a situation. So you miss out in life. It becomes a self-
fulfilling prophecy.

'I won't book tickets for that outdoor Shakespeare
event – it'll probably rain, April's such an

unpredictable month.'

'I'll give that networking event a miss, I think, I've never met anybody interesting at any one I've been to yet.'

Predictions are turned into *facts*.

## CATASTROPHISING

Catastrophising is a tendency to exaggerate the consequences of an action. Highly anxious or stressed people are prime candidates for this mode of thinking.

A highly active imagination tinged with clairvoyancy results in a belief that disaster is inevitable (remember Jane in Session 2?). Albert Ellis termed this type of thinking 'awfulising'. Unpleasant situations are upgraded in a person's mind as being awful or catastrophic whether they've happened or you think they will happen. It's an inappropriate assessment of the circumstances which results in unwarranted upset or distress over a situation.

'After the takeover they're bound to trim staff in the department. I'll be one of the first to be turfed out. It could take months, even years, for me to find something new.'

We need to be aware of when we're engaging in this type of thinking, even when in the midst of problems. They can be made more catastrophic than the situation warrants.

## LABELLING

You'll recognise this distorted thinking habit immediately. It's something we all do frequently. We attach a description to ourselves or other people. And as we know, words have power.

You may recognise some labels from childhood days that came from other children, your parents or other authority figures. Equally there may be terms that stuck with you and you find yourself using them even now.

Let's look at a few negative terms that you may find yourself using about yourself and others. How about we start with that good old favourite, failure? Hopeless. Thoughtless. Useless. Stupid. Lazy. Bossy. Aggressive. Immature. Insensitive. Weak. Arrogant... Quite a list.

The point is, other people, or ourselves, may well be one or (if we're unlucky!) all of these things. But what we ought to be doing is trying to separate a person's *behaviours* from the person as a whole. Usually it's not the character of the person that is causing us problems; it's their thinking and/or behaviour. Only by recognising this can we feel motivated to try and improve the relationship by communicating in a different way.

These emotionally charged words – for example labelling somebody as irresponsible – may generate feelings of anger within you, which may provoke reciprocal treatment. When you label yourself, other people or events in a negative way these emotionally charged words may steer you towards engaging in adverse behaviour. People object to their whole identity being classified by a label.

When we apply labels to ourselves, either as self-talk or voiced as a statement like, 'I'm hopeless', 'That's pathetic', 'What a moron', it often has a debilitating effect on the mind. Accept your substandard behaviour as single actions. Separate what you did from the *self.* Otherwise the mind can't work on improvement.

## SHOULD/MUST (RIGID THINKING)

Albert Ellis showed that a lot of our problems arise when we use imperatives: those words like *should, must* and *ought.* He spoke of this dysfunction as the 'must' level – a situation where we add another level of belief by using these words, resulting in statements we tell ourselves to make us feel even worse. It's a common thinking pattern that is responsible for a lot of guilt in our lives.

We insist that the world, or situations, or things, or people, 'should' or 'must' be a certain way. The result is anger and frustration. Also in this category we can put 'ought' and 'have to'.

'I should be married by now.'

'I should have achieved more in life than this.'

'I should be more appreciated.'

'I should have been more supportive.'

'I must get in touch with Kristina.'

'I must clear out the spare room.'

'I ought to have lost weight by now.'
'I ought to be more considerate about . . .'

Very few of us do not hold some of these rigid beliefs. I should be like this; the world should be like this; other people should behave like this. We set ourselves up for misery if we hold these rigid beliefs about how we, people and the world should be.

The healthy approach to thinking is to eliminate the thought that things should or must be a certain way – we need to think in terms of *preferences*. Our beliefs will not cause a problem if we think of them as desires and realise that things do not have to unfold in a certain way. The healthy way of thinking is to eliminate the mindset of demanding and to *prefer* that: things should be a certain way; people should behave in a certain way; they should treat us in a certain way. At the same time, we build in a flexibility to cope when things don't happen this way.

Just a quick point for clarity. We have situations where, when we use the 'should', it means 'so that I can'. This is a 'conditional' should, as in 'We should aim to leave the house by 8.15 to get to the surgery by 9.00.' Or 'I shouldn't have a drink tonight so that I can be sure of feeling fresh for the interview tomorrow morning.'

It's the *unconditional* shoulds that cause problems.

All of these types of irrational thinking errors tend to become habits based on our rigid beliefs and, unless they are brought to our attention, become something that is repeated time and time again in everyday life.

## COFFEE BREAK

A heart surgeon used to take his car for regular servicing to a nearby garage. He would exchange pleasantries with the owner who was a highly skilled, overworked, but not very wealthy mechanic.

'I need to know something,' the mechanic said to him one day. 'It's been worrying me for years. I keep trying to come to terms with it, but I go round in circles.'

'Oh,' replied the heart surgeon, looking extremely concerned. 'Is it something related to your health?'

'No, no. Please don't take this the wrong way. I've been thinking about what we both do for a living and how much more you get paid than I do.'

'Yes?' the heart surgeon replied.

'Take a look at this,' the mechanic said as he pointed towards an engine he was working on.

'The customer brings it in to me to check how it's running, 'cos he thinks there's a problem, then leaves it with me. Next day, I open it up, I fix the valves and put it all back together again so it works as good as new. We basically do the same job, don't we?'

'In a way,' the surgeon replied.

'But you get paid about ten times or more than what I get,' the mechanic replied. 'How do you explain that?'

The surgeon paused and then smiled and replied, 'Try it with the engine running.'

# Tame that Anger

## It's the tip of the 'iceberg'

*Anger: an acid that can do more harm to the vessel in which it is stored than to anything on which it is poured.*
DE IRA (ON ANGER) SENECA (C. AD 45)

As we've discussed earlier, it's not other people that make you feel something. Anger is an emotion and when you're feeling it, it's *your* emotion. You may blame other people for triggering your anger, but it's still *your* anger. And there's a difference between *being* angry and *behaving* angrily. The problem of anger lies with you, whether you're displaying it with your behaviour or experiencing it internally.

You'll hear people say, 'I can't help it, I'm an angry person.' But it's not a personality thing; it a habit, stemming from your view or perceptions about life and how you deal with your emotions. The good news is that habits can be changed. You can analyse and change your thinking with the ABC model until it becomes quite natural for you.

Just like stress, anger can be useful in some situations. A lot of the time we are right to feel angry, but it's how you deal with your anger – either in an assertive way or an unhealthy way – that matters. You can express anger in healthy, constructive ways. You can often articulate your anger much more effectively with some grace. After all, in some situations it can be a positive emotion.

You may come across some people who barely exhibit anger. Although on the surface they may appear psychologically well adjusted and able to cope with situations calmly, this is not always a good thing. They may be suppressing their anger which leaves them dissatisfied; in addition they may display more passive-aggressive tendencies. In their relationships with others both in and out of work they may be inclined to behave unassertively.

This compounds the situation, leading to more dissatisfaction. The point is that some element of anger helps to motivate us for a particular cause, and also to stand up for ourselves in a conflict situation.

We need to address how we express that anger. Recognising when the 'fuse' has been well and truly lit, with the physiological signs of the rapid heartbeat, the shaking hands and the jaw movements, means it's time to take a check.

What are the thoughts and beliefs that are lighting the fuse (the B in our ABC model)? What are the likely consequences if you carry on acting this way (the C in our ABC model)? Will it stop you achieving your 'goal' or make for an unpleasant outcome? For example, it might prevent you being considered for promotion, or ruin the lunch that you're attending.

If you dispute the B with more realistic thinking, how will it change the C? You may still have a chance for that work promotion or enjoy a pleasant lunch with no conflict.

Look at what Marcus Aurelius felt he had to look forward to when he rose for the day:

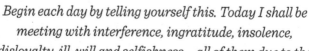

*Begin each day by telling yourself this. Today I shall be meeting with interference, ingratitude, insolence, disloyalty, ill-will and selfishness – all of them due to the offenders' ignorance of what is good and evil.*
*MEDITATIONS* MARCUS AURELIUS (*C.* AD 171–5)

## Anger and our underlying emotions

Anger is probably the hardest emotion we feel that we're able to control. We're always being told that suppressing or 'bottling up' anger is detrimental to our emotional and physical health.

Yet it's something that most of us are guilty of. How often have you, or other people you've observed, fallen into the 'I'm fine' category, for example. Two simple words often used to mask our angry feelings – a passive-aggressive response to a question.

'Are you sure you're OK about picking up Hayley,
because I've got my snooker competition?'
'Yes, *I'm fine.*'

'Are you feeling better after clearing the air with the departmental head this morning?' 'Yes, I did it, I'm fine.'

Often meaningful conversations are lost and relationships become fractured when the words are taken at their face value. This suppression of inward anger often exposes itself later.

We can try and avoid situations that make us angry, but that's not a long-term solution for dealing with anger issues. Therefore, we need to find healthier ways of expressing anger, as well as examining our way of thinking.

Ongoing research into stress and anger shows that people who are continually working to a deadline and may also be working long hours may be prone to frequent episodes of anger. In addition, people who don't trust that others can do a job as well as them will inevitably overburden themselves with more responsibilities. Sometimes this may be down to 'perfectionist' tendencies, but in other instances it may be a competence or 'control' issue.

It's our beliefs leading to our thinking that causes our tension. So once again we're back to the ABC model.

Try to identify emotions that might be causing your anger. Most of us are guilty of not being aware of what triggers our feelings and emotions. We're aware that anger is a powerful emotion in its own right, but we never think to analyse what the *reason* for our tension may be.

There's an interesting concept of the 'anger iceberg' which suggests that beneath the surface we have many other hidden emotions. These include feelings such as guilt, insecurity, hurt, fear, shame, sadness, embarrassment or a combination of a number of them, all of which may make a person feel vulnerable.

Investigating what lies beneath the surface enables you to work out what is causing the anger that is on show. In other words, what underlying emotions your anger is masking.

Equally, when anger is directed at you, it encourages you to

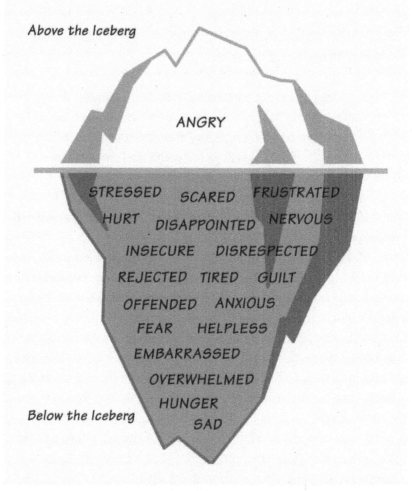

Above the Iceberg

ANGRY

STRESSED   SCARED   FRUSTRATED
HURT   DISAPPOINTED   NERVOUS
INSECURE   DISRESPECTED
REJECTED   TIRED   GUILT
OFFENDED   ANXIOUS
FEAR   HELPLESS
EMBARRASSED
OVERWHELMED
HUNGER
Below the Iceberg         SAD

dig deeper so that you might understand better and manage your reactions accordingly. So anger is, more often than not, disguising other unexpressed emotions. In relationships the awareness of 'below-the-surface' emotions is extremely important. The tip of the iceberg is really the symptom, not the cause.

When you change your irrational beliefs, you're on the path to improving your mental health. A lot of what we experience in our day-to-day living – that may manifest itself unhealthily as anger – could, with a change of thinking, be 'downgraded' to a healthier and less destructive emotion. How about annoyance or exasperation or frustration? More often than not, what we're perceiving as anger is in fact not 'true' anger, but stress.

> 'No, Sarah, I do not want to listen to that documentary now. As I said before, I don't care how interesting it is; I just want to be left alone for fifteen minutes to make some calls. You'll be really pleased if I don't manage to get an emergency call out for the drains.'

This is a person who is stressed. Anger is his way of *conveying* it.

So we're in a situation in life where we are enduring acute or chronic stress and therefore we're having frequent outbursts of anger, which causes more stress. More stress causes more anger. It's a vicious circle.

All research shows that stress is more prevalent today than in recent years, and certainly it receives more media coverage. We're also being told there is more anger in society and it is highly likely that, for those people prone to anger, this increase in stress contributes to the increase in angry behaviours.

We know about 'triggers' that arouse angry feelings and the 'activator', the A in the ABC model. We all have feelings and emotions below the 'iceberg' that tip us over.

The result is that the severity of the anger may be inappropriate to the situation. Quite often, what we're really wanting is something specific: an acknowledgement of some sort or an apology, for example. Think of situations you've observed where an angry outburst jeopardised a person's ultimate aim and they ended up being the one that had to do the apologising (instead of the 'guilty' party).

The Oscars in Los Angeles in 2022 springs to mind, which was overshadowed completely by one of the subsequent winners having to apologise to a shocked audience for his behaviour, in an incident of violence that was screened live around the globe.

Put a rein on those automatic emotional thoughts in the heat of the moment and ask yourself what might be the best way to respond. It's far better than letting yourself engage in impulsive and irreversible responses that can lead to long-term regrets. There is a saying: 'I stop and taste my words before I let them pass my teeth.'

## Your physical health

When our tolerance level drops in any situation there's more chance of being tipped over the line, resulting in an angry outburst.

Quite often our own physical health is the catalyst for the anger trigger. Being unwell, or suffering from poor sleep or general tiredness, for example, can set the process off. If you're a regular traveller, you've probably observed spontaneous anger with airline check-in staff, as tired travellers are informed of flight disruptions. This invariably results in more stress as you're having to deal with the discord that your anger may create.

Sometimes, it's more productive and less damaging, when you're engaging in an awkward conversation or in the midst of a frustrating event, to remember the benefits of a little pause. As we learned in Session 2, breathing well is really important at such a time. Try breathing deeply and slowly – around eight breaths a minute – to slow your heartbeat and help you feel more relaxed.

We know that personal stress levels will be a factor in determining your predisposition to frequent angry altercations or long-term anger. We've also seen how we have a choice regarding how to interpret situations. We encounter many daily situations where the 'adversity' or 'activator' – the 'A' – allows us an opportunity to be angry or hostile. But we can decide whether we want to take up that opportunity.

## Two types of anger

Our subjective view of the world will differ widely from other people's. They have their own 'reality' and we have ours. Indeed, there is no such thing as reality – only perception.

A lot of anger that is a part of people's lives falls under the two categories of long-lasting anger or transient anger.

**Transient anger** is usually activated by some kind of situation, and things often calm down very quickly.

Some people are prone to getting angry more easily and also more intensely than the average person. They can be described in cognitive terms as having 'low frustration tolerance' (LFT).

With anger there are often 'should' demands that serve to distort the importance of an event being experienced. These people don't feel they 'should' have to wait that long at the supermarket checkout, or experience a train delay, or have a mobile phone with a battery that has inconveniently just run out.

When we're dealing with strangers in day-to-day interactions we experience many possible triggers that will lead to transient anger. The shop assistant who takes too long to acknowledge and serve you, the customer, because she has to finish telling a story to her colleague about the blind date she went on the previous evening. The waiter who seems incapable of looking beyond one table to see if other customers need attention or are waiting for the bill. The taxi driver who takes you on a 'magical mystery tour' to get to you home.

By contrast, when we look at **long-lasting anger**, the root cause is usually an unhealthy and 'distorted' way of thinking.

We have expectations about other people and our thinking can get exaggerated when it comes to others' misdemeanours. We hold them to high standards and think about how they should have behaved in a different way – thoughts that lead you down the path of constant ruminating ('She said . . .', 'Then I said . . .', 'Then guess what she said to that . . .', 'And then she had the nerve to . . .').

This long-lasting anger results in resentments that can

endure for years or even an entire lifetime. Often only a change of thinking can bring a person out of that spiral that constantly leads to the same thought destination. The mind doesn't do *positive* spiralling. The spiral is always downwards, and negative thoughts win the battle.

How many people do you know who are in this position? Holding on to their lifelong memories and feuds – feeling good and feeling bad at the same time?

Feeling *good* that they're not letting the person off for their past behaviour and transgressions. ('That will teach them to . . .', 'Well it's their loss because now they won't be able to . . .'). But also feeling *bad* at the effect it has had on their life and their mental health. ('Sometimes I wake up at night – I have dreams and think about it. It just goes round and round in my head, and I feel emotional and exhausted from the lack of sleep'; 'We've deprived ourselves of a friendship – that makes me sad as well as angry, what a waste of life.')

If we think back to the ABC framework, of course it's other people's actions (the A) that are responsible for our anger, but it's how we choose to perceive things (the B) that determines our reactions. 'But isn't it you who's suffering by holding on to the anger?'

Scientists have observed that anger differs from all our other unhealthy emotions in the way that we exhibit the tendency not to want to let it go. Our sense of justice at certain times may be so intense that we want to continue with those feelings and not let the other person (or thing) 'get away with it'.

But, of course, not all anger is a bad thing. As well as anger that is felt about other people we come into contact with, we can cite a list where we feel long-lasting anger against the world in general: organisations, situations, politicians. If we didn't feel angry about things at times, then we wouldn't have the motivation to try to change anything. If the anger is appropriate for a particular situation and is expressed in the right way, for the right reasons, it can act as a motivator, is valid and furthers a cause.

If we just take government and politicians, the amount of newsprint and television coverage that provides a forum for angry and satirical comment is huge. I remember a radio series which used to trail with the following: 'The show that does for politicians what the guillotine did for sore throats.'

We hold certain expectations about people and the world; people should, or should not, behave in a particular way. Quite naturally it's other people's actions that are the 'activators' (the **A**) for our anger. But, as we know only too well, it's our reactions that count – how we choose to perceive things based on our beliefs (the **B**).

Criticism, whether directed at ourselves or other people, isn't always the best way of effecting a change for the better. Have you noticed that, with animals and children, you get the best result in trying to get them to do something or behave differently if they're 'rewarded' in some way?

Usually discord or conflict has more chance of a solution or being resolved if the interaction remains conversational. You see people having explosive arguments about things which are beyond their control. You may have heard it said: 'The thing I hate about an argument is that it always interrupts a discussion.'

As mentioned earlier, arguments relating to certain topics, for example politics, are futile and time-wasting. So much more can be achieved with an acceptance of being able to 'agree to disagree' – and also maybe the injection of a little light humour. For example, wasn't Aesop right when he observed:

*We hang the petty thieves and appoint the great ones to*
*public office.*
*AESOP'S FABLES* AESOP (SIXTH CENTURY BC)

When we encounter a situation that we feel violates our expectations of how things *should* be or how people *should* behave, remember that we can choose whether to respond with anger or experience angry feelings. It's back to that word again: control. We do have control and therefore we're able to influence the emotions we feel.

In many instances we are programmed to believe that others 'should' behave in a certain way; in accordance with the way that we think and believe they should. This rigid way of thinking ensures that, faced with a situation, we find it very difficult to manage our emotions as we quickly lose control in the moment.

As we know from the ABC model, there is a sequence in our thoughts, feelings, action process. As Albert Ellis observed when formulating his therapy, most people do not spend enough time thinking about the way they think. As he continually reminded people, you feel the way you think.

Let me show you a way of illustrating how the cycle of spiralling thoughts can be halted when we gradually learn how to 'watch' our thinking. Bring to mind a stressful situation from the past, or something that you feel acts as a trigger for a possible episode of anger on your part. It often helps if you close your eyes and create that story in your mind for about three to five minutes.

How did you behave? What were the thoughts that were going through your mind? Could you have handled it differently? How would a change of thinking have changed the outcome?

## THE STOICS AND ANGER
As we've learnt, and as the Stoics have reminded us, we're able to control our feelings by controlling our *thinking*. Unfortunately, most people's automatic thoughts in a potentially anger-inducing situation tend to be neither rational nor helpful. A cool and rational internal assessment could bring the temperature down, but instead, we become slaves to our emotions. It's easier.

You'll remember that for the Stoics, the 'passions' were the root cause of our suffering:

*A real man doesn't give way to anger and discontent...*
*And such a person has strength, courage and endurance*
*– unlike the angry and the complaining.*
*MEDITATIONS* MARCUS AURELIUS (*C.* AD 171–5)

The Stoics believed that anger robs you of precious energy and so it is better to exhibit non-reactivity when faced with something that is probably beyond your control.

- When you *react* to feelings of anger you are *out of control.*

- When you *respond* to feelings of anger you are *in control.*

What's the psychology behind this? When you respond *you* are controlling the mind instead of the *mind* controlling you.

- When you *react* to feelings of anger you're engaging in a *reflex* action.

- When you *respond* to feelings of anger you're engaging in *thinking.*

Our autonomic nervous system makes an assessment of any impending threat or danger and our intuitive reaction to a particular situation may generate feelings of anger and hostility. Aim to get your parasympathetic nervous system (PSN) going (the opposite of 'fight or flight', and which is sometimes known as 'rest and digest') which will lead to a calmer state of affairs.

At one of my workshops I was told about an episode one of the delegates had experienced. She had gone to the department store to pick up a 'click and collect' item. Although she had a text to say it would be available after 2.30, it wasn't there when she arrived at the counter at 3.05pm. She flew into a rage, saying that 'service had deteriorated'. There was a queue building up and she asked for the manager.

He took her to one side for a little privacy and explained that the particular delivery van had been involved in an accident. She still shouted at him, saying, 'Why can't you organise back-up if that happens?' He explained that it had only happened around ninety minutes ago.

He repeated twice that as a 'gesture' they would deliver it to her by special taxi by 6pm at the latest, but she didn't respond to the statement and kept going on about 'bad service' and having 'back-up'.

Finally, he repeated to her that they would arrange delivery in a taxi by 6pm at the latest. She calmed down a little and said: 'Well, if you'd have offered to do that earlier in our conversation . . .' Memory often suffers during tense and angry moments and periods of stress.

How urgently did she need this consignment in reality? What was the product in question?

A wall-mounted coffee mug holder!

As the classical Greek philosopher Aristotle observed all that time ago:

*Anybody can become angry – that is easy, but to be angry with the right person and to the right degree at the right time and for the right purpose, and in the right way – that is not within everybody's power and is not easy.*
THE ART OF RHETORIC ARISTOTLE (c. 384–322 BC)

I'm sure we can all recall situations when one or more of these factors was not quite 'right'.

## IRRATIONAL ANGER

Albert Ellis felt the core problem in anger management was that we mostly insist that things are worse than they are. He noted the tendency for people to regard things as 'catastrophic' and accepted that things can get bad, but they are rarely catastrophic, and consequently we make ourselves miserable unnecessarily. To counteract this he urged his clients and delegates to look at their irrational core beliefs and modify their thinking and see whether anger is justified.

A lot of life's interpersonal problems stem from the feeling of the need to be 'right'. (Have you noticed how difficult it is to argue with someone who is not obsessed with being right?) Relationships become fractured, and long-standing feuds entrenched. Try to gauge the other person's perspective on the situation that makes them think the way they do.

See if you can adapt your thinking and observe, in a moment of anger, whether your beliefs are rational or irrational. You may find it hard to forgive someone for something that happened, which results in you remaining angry and unforgiving. For example, those words that somebody uttered to you in a tense and angry encounter, which they now regret and wish they could take back. As Paul McCartney reminds us in a song, after we've said something we regret, how we long for yesterday so that we can go back and change our words.

Sometimes you have to make a decision about what's important to you. In some 'interpersonal' issues, at the end of the day, are *people* more important than your *principles* in this particular conflict? It's possible you may be right about the point in question, but if you're dealing with someone who's *convinced* of their own opinion, is it always worth the agony?

There's often much hurt caused by a misunderstanding of what may have been said to us because of the *meaning* we derive from the words that have been spoken (and in the opposite situation, words we have said). We know how powerful words are. Anger can act as a protective 'shield', because in many cases it feels better than being sad or hurt. (Remember the 'anger iceberg'.) Sometimes an acceptance and an apology may be the only way to break the impasse.

Seneca was exiled to Corsica by the Emperor Claudius, and while he was there he wrote a book on anger. He put it like this, when he looked at much of the anger that people exhibit:

*... our anger invariably lasts longer than the damage done to us.*
*DE IRA (ON ANGER) SENECA (C. AD 45)*

He noted that often anger arises out of a misunderstanding or a misperception of reality. So he spent his time writing about ways of preventing anger in the first instance. He admonished his citizens by advising them that:

*... the best plan is to reject straightaway the first incentives to anger, to resist its very beginnings and to take care not to be betrayed by it.*

Recognising its effects on our mental health, he continued:

*...for if once it begins to carry us away it is hard to get back again into a healthy condition because reason goes for nothing when once passion has been admitted into the mind.*

Seneca reminds us of the thoughts-feelings-behaviour process that he and his fellow philosophers documented. He advises:

*...turn all anger's indications into their opposites... We should force ourselves to relax our face, soften our voice, and slow our pace of walking. If we do this, our internal state will come to resemble our external state and our anger will have dissipated.*

He was really telling us about our parasympathetic nervous system (the opposite of fight or flight), which is stimulated by deep breaths from the stomach area that increase oxygen flow to the angry brain, promoting calmness.

Furthermore he advocates a more helpful attitude towards our mental well-being when he wisely suggests that we take

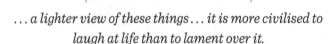

*...a lighter view of these things... it is more civilised to laugh at life than to lament over it.*

## BECOMING A BETTER PERSON

Seneca felt there was a blueprint as to how we should live our lives and how we should aim to relate to other people, which is hard to disagree with. 'Life is too short to waste it being angry.'

He went on to advise:

*Make yourself a person to be loved by all while you live and missed when you have made your departure.*
DE IRA (ON ANGER) SENECA (C. AD 45)

The Stoics felt that we should keep an open mind before assessing others and not think the worst, as it affects you and how you view and trust the world. They felt we should strive to become better people, virtuous in the ancient sense of the word.

We know that we unconsciously mirror what we observe when meeting others. For example, if you look enthusiastic and pleased, it often results in them mirroring that behaviour. We can all learn things from people we meet and, as the Stoics said, treating each other with kindness is a skill. But they didn't mean that you should always be compliant if people then treat you badly.

I like actress Joanna Lumley's comments during an interview, which the ancient Stoics would probably have approved of:

'The secret, darling, is to love everyone you meet. From the moment you meet them. Give everyone the benefit of the doubt. Start from a position that they are lovely and that you will love them. Most people will respond to that and be lovely and love you back, and it becomes a self-fulfilling prophecy, and then you can achieve the most wonderful things.'

It's the last sentence that I particularly like:

'But get rid of any of the bastards that let you down.'
*IF I COULD TELL YOU JUST ONE THING* RICHARD REED
(2016)

---

## COFFEE BREAK

Turning up at JFK International Airport to find his flight delayed, the tired businessman went to the airport shop, bought what seemed an interesting book, a large coffee and a small packet of biscuits containing five double chocolate chip cookies.

It was crowded at the cafeteria but he found a seat at a table next to a lady. 'Would you mind if I . . .?' he said, pointing at the vacant seat.

'Of course,' she replied.

After a few minutes' reading he became absorbed in the book, took one chocolate chip cookie out of the pack and then took a swig of coffee.

To his surprise the lady next to him calmly took one of the cookies from the pack and ate it.

He was stunned but couldn't bring himself to say anything or to even look at her.

He rather awkwardly carried on reading his book and reached over and took out another cookie and ate it.

Shortly after, the lady reached over and took another cookie. By now the anger was beginning to build up in him.

Then, to make matters worse, to his amazement she picked up the packet, stared at him and offered him the last cookie.

That was it, he stood up. 'Absolutely ridiculous,' he shouted out. 'I've never seen anything like it!' He angrily picked up his hand luggage, glared at the lady and strode off to the

---

departure gate check-in as the flight was nearly ready for boarding.

He reached into his bag for his boarding pass, dropping an unopened pack of double chocolate chip cookies!

# The Gods May Throw the Dice

## You've played all your cards

*Live not as though there were a thousand years ahead of
you. Fate is at your elbow; make yourself good while life
and power are still yours.*
*MEDITATIONS* MARCUS AURELIUS (*C.* AD 171–5)

Much of our daily agony derives from a lack of acceptance of the circumstances we're experiencing. There's a mismatch between what we expect and what is actually happening.

As the ancients reminded us, things that we cannot control do not warrant wasted energy and the associated frustration that it brings. We don't want to spend time fighting reality just because we feel things are unfair and 'shouldn't' be the way they have turned out. All easier said than done, of course, but if we're able to develop an acceptance of what's happening in life we spend less of our precious time experiencing angst and being in a stressful state.

The Stoics would advocate that we avoid ruminating on the past and be philosophical about our circumstances. Maybe there is a reason or some higher purpose that decrees that this is the way it is meant to be.

They weren't fatalistic about the future; on the contrary, they spent much of their time trying to influence future outcomes. But they also greeted what came their way with acceptance.

*Don't hope that events will turn out the way you want, welcome events in whichever way they happen. This is the path to peace.*
ENCHIRIDION EPICTETUS (C. AD 125)

Demanding of the universe, 'Why is this happening to me?', 'This is so unfair', 'Life shouldn't be like this' all serve to feed on those feelings of sadness, anger, anxiety and bitterness.

Seneca had this to say:

*For the wise man does not consider himself unworthy of any gifts from Fortune's hands.*

However, he wisely reminds us to be on our guard, as:

*Misfortune weighs most heavily on those who expect nothing but good fortune.*
*ON THE HAPPY LIFE* SENECA (*C.* AD 58)

We spoke about the importance of acceptance earlier on and how we should accept 'what is' – in other words let go of any expectations of how things should be. If we spend our time cursing ourselves for not behaving in a certain way, we're taking away the one thing that we can control: the power to alter our thinking. We need to let go of wishing that our past had been different.

It doesn't mean that you're giving up, or that you're in favour of what is happening to you, or that you don't regret a decision you made which turned out to be far from perfect. You're recognising that you don't have control over events, reclaiming energy that was previously spent on resisting, and at the same time bringing clarity to enable you to focus on possible options.

Think of how much energy is wasted – all that anger and frustration – when you spend your time 'wishing' that things could have been different. We all do this. We devise stories of how different life might be had we been dealt a different hand of cards. All that mental energy you expend wandering in the *land of what could have been.* 'I could have done this', 'I should have done that', 'She could have done this . . .'

We're back to the stories we tell ourselves. 'If only I'd bought that other house.' 'If only I'd taken that other job.' 'I should have married.' 'We'd have been much better off doing ...' All those self-critical statements that tell us how much better our life might have been if we'd made alternative decisions. All that mental energy spent on daydreaming and regret and the loss of potential happiness and life fulfilment. But how do we know that? How can we possibly know?

Unfavourable decisions and actions we made in the past will always seem so obvious when we examine them in the present. That same energy might be better utilised actually trying to devise a way of achieving the life circumstances that you would prefer.

Then we may indulge in the dreaded 'compare and despair'. It's natural that you will compare yourself, your achievements and your life situation with other people. There will always be differences in material wealth and individual life circumstances between ourselves and other people.

We have to remember, for better or worse, that all our life experiences to date – in other words all the things that have happened to us – have 'forged' who we are today. We would not be the person who we are without those experiences. If those alternative experiences from the 'land of what could have been' had happened, you would not be *you*.

Marcus Aurelius wrote that a good man will welcome

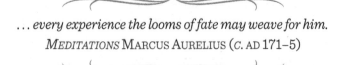

*... every experience the looms of fate may weave for him.*
*MEDITATIONS* MARCUS AURELIUS (*C.* AD 171–5)

## Luck and 'pluck'

In anything we pursue, luck will always be a factor as we confront the inevitable fact that chance plays a huge part in determining life's outcomes.

We can't just rely on our skills and talents, however, these are important in determining our success. They give us the edge over others less skilled than us in situations, allowing us to see things and do things that others may not. When luck or chance is not working for us, our skills and talents may then lessen the impact of the damage caused.

We can look at different types of luck, which may help us evaluate the degree of control we have and be less critical of ourselves. Random good luck is something we cannot control. Think, for example, of the lucky raffle ticket or lottery winner. Random bad luck is, again, something out of our control – a flat tyre, roof tiles blowing off in a storm. Then we have what is often termed 'opportunistic' luck, which is luck that you help create – good returns on your carefully chosen stocks and shares, increased sales of your service after a promotional campaign.

We can understand life better if we observe people and situations and remember that old phrase 'luck and pluck'. It refers to the difference between those people who seem to effortlessly obtain what they want through good fortune (luck) or illegitimate means, and the people who have to make their way in life through hard efforts (pluck). We can define pluck as 'courage or resolution in the face of difficulties'.

Perhaps we can add our own symbolism to this phrase by noting the addition of the 'p' that turns luck into pluck. Maybe we could call this 'p' *persistence*. So if 'the Gods' don't favour us with good fortune and we've played all our cards, we use our persistence in the hope, next time, of being dealt a better hand and obtaining some luck.

### Try to shape your destiny

We've spent the last sessions highlighting how so much in life is out of our control. With all our talent, time sacrifice and imagination, we can still be thwarted in achieving our goals. Then we often engage in self-criticism as we stare at failure. Only when we recognise and accept that we also need that vital 'ingredient' of luck in the mix, can things turn out right.

Paul J. Getty, a man who knew a thing or two about luck, was asked to what he attributed his immense wealth. He said, 'Some people find oil, others don't.'

So we carry on in life accepting setbacks as they occur. We know that we can't control our destiny. But with our persistence and skill there is something we can do, despite the Gods throwing the 'dice' – we carry on trying to 'shape' our destiny.

You've probably come across people who refuse to 'fold' when things don't go their way. You may have a certain degree of admiration for them. We also see and hear the stories of people in popular culture, sport, entertainment and the business world. J.K. Rowling expressed it well in her Harvard speech in 2008:

'It is impossible to live without failing at something unless you live so cautiously that you might as well not have lived at all ... Failure gave me an inner security that I had never obtained by passing examinations ... Failure taught me things that I could not have learned any other way. I discovered I had a strong will and more discipline than I had suspected.'

Elvis Presley's early performance at the Grand Ole Oprey, the famous home of country music in Nashville, Tennessee, in 1954, went down so badly with the audience that he was famously told by manager Jim Denny: 'You ain't going nowhere, son. You should go back to driving a truck.' Elvis had enough self-belief and self-confidence to persist and eventually became known as the 'King of Rock 'n' Roll'.

It's so easy to give up when failure looms in your thinking – but for inspiration take a look at the world of sport. Here it's not enough to be competent in the three primary areas – physical, tactical and technical. Add to these the fourth essential element: psychological. We've discussed earlier the tendency to look at the past and the future to the detriment of the present. It's no different in competition. The important thing for players is 'focus' – on the present. That's all there is. If the focus goes, often the match goes.

More than any other, tennis is the sport in which the 'mental' side of the game is paramount. I still marvel at the mental resilience and focus shown by Rafael Nadal when I recall the Australian Open Final in January 2022, a match that had theatre and brilliance of play, which left audiences spellbound.

With a record twenty Grand Slam titles to his name (sharing that distinction with two other players), this was an opportunity for Nadal to become the first male tennis player ever to win twenty-one Grand Slams. He faced a few problems, though. He'd been out of the game for six months with no match play, due to his chronic and recurring foot injury. A month before, the thirty-five-year-old player had been contemplating with his manager the possibility that his career was over – retirement from the game a likely outcome.

Now he had surprised himself and the tennis world by reaching the final. His opponent, Daniil Medvedev, ten years his junior, took the first set. Nadal led 4-1 in the second set – not before enduring forty-shot rallies – then served for the set at 5-3 and failed to take his set point. The set went to a tie-break that his opponent won.

Nadal was two sets down. An uphill task for anybody. He could have looked to the despair of the past or the hopelessness of the future. But he had the mental strength to choose to focus on the present. Facing three break points in the sixth game of the third set it looked as though it would all be over, but Nadal took the set 6-4. He was back in the game – for now.

It was the start of a fightback. But he still needed to take the next two sets. At the stroke of midnight Nadal closed out the fourth set. Was there to be a Cinderella ending? The score was now two sets all, so he'd managed to haul himself up to a deciding fifth set.

With gripping tension on the court and a vociferous crowd in the arena, Nadal got himself up to a 5-4 position and then failed to serve out the match. More indescribable tension as the Spaniard somehow found the mental strength to break his opponent's serve to go ahead 6-5, and then went on to take the set 7-5, to win his twenty-first record-breaking Grand Slam after a gruelling 5 hours and 23 minutes.

This was the second-longest Grand Slam final of all time. The other one? A 2012 final in Australia lasting 5 hours and 53 minutes between Novak Djokovic and – *déjà vu* – Rafael Nadal!

It would have been easy for Nadal to convince himself that luck was against him. That, despite the odds, he had at least managed to make it to the final. But what made him carry on was convincing himself that his skill and talents could turn things around.

It's something we must all strive to do when luck or those 'cards' seem to be stacked against us. It motivates us to carry on rather than give up. How often do we give in to those doubting voices about failure and not being good enough when we encounter a setback?

As human beings we have our own subjective opinion in how we make sense of the world and view the vagaries and challenges of everyday living. This attitude or belief is what determines our psychological response to circumstances.

I remember somebody saying something quite inspirational in my early years: 'If you *want* to do something, you find a way. If you *don't* want to do something you find an excuse.'

## COFFEE BREAK

John felt out of control in his life, and not for the first time. His work consisted of dealing with one relentless problem after another. He was keen to help people and that resulted in more requests for his time.

Quite often he wanted to say 'no', but he found it difficult as he felt he was letting people down. The result was that his days were stressful, and as soon as he tackled things on his 'priority' list, more items would appear. So he never felt as though he'd made any progress.

He wanted to see more of his family – his children were growing up in his absence, he felt. He also wanted to have time to renew the relationships that had fallen by the wayside, and to resume those hobbies that made life worth living.

He thought that after getting the little things sorted out, he would have time for the 'big' things in his life that mattered to him. But days and weeks came and went, and then the years too.

One day he came across a flyer for a talk at a nearby concert hall. A philosopher was giving a talk, titled 'Living the FULL life you want'.

He went along on the day and felt relief as he found the auditorium was packed.

The philosopher walked onto the stage carrying a large tray. On the tray was a very large glass jar, a bag containing some rocks about three inches long, a bag of pebbles, a small container of sand, two coffee cups and a cafetière. 'Good evening, all,' she said. 'You're all looking intrigued about my props. Don't worry, it will all become clear. They are the key to your more fulfilling life.'

She put the jar down on the table. Then she placed all the rocks into the jar, right up to the rim. She held the jar up to the audience and then asked, 'Is it full?'

The audience agreed that there was no room for any more rocks, so responded, 'Yes.'

She then picked up the bag of small pebbles and poured these into the jar. The philosopher started to shake the jar. The pebbles trickled down and filled up the space around the big rocks. 'Is it now full?' she asked.

Members of the audience looked at each other. Again they responded, 'Yes'.

'Is it really full?' she asked.

The philosopher then picked up the tub of sand. She poured the sand in between the pebbles and the rocks, shaking it up so that the sand would seep its way into the remaining gaps. She then held the jar up to the audience showing how it was even fuller than before.

John, who had been sitting quietly in the front row, felt moved to shout out to the philosopher, 'Yes, now it's really full.' The audience applauded their agreement.

'I need all of you to be aware that this jar represents your life,' the philosopher said, as she sat down on her stool.

'The rocks represent the important things – your family, friends, your passions and your physical and mental health. If you lost everything else and had these things alone, your life would be full.

'These pebbles represent things that matter to you, like your home and your job. The sand represents everything else – the small stuff.

'If you put the big things first, the little things fit around them, finding their way into the gaps.'

She produced another empty jar and filled it nearly to the

*No space for the rocks in your life if you fill the jar with pebbles and sand first*

top with just sand. She tried to put a few rocks into the jar; one just rested on the top while the others fell to the floor.

'If you fill the jar with sand first, there's no room for any rocks and pebbles.

'In life if you spend all your time and energy on little things, there won't be any room left for those things that are really *important* to you.

'So live a life where you pay attention to the things that bring you *real* happiness and fulfilment. Make sure you're

*The 'Full' Jar of Life*

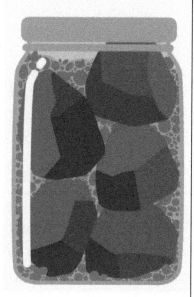

realistic with your priorities. Give your children your time, take your partner out for dinner, take time to talk to the people that count and make time to read a good book.

'Take care of the rocks first. The things that truly matter. The rest is just sand.'

While the audience applauded, the philosopher poured two cups of coffee from a cafetière. She then poured each cup into the full jar and the liquid seeped through the rocks, pebbles and sand with no apparent effort.

The audience continued their applause. A girl raised her hand. 'What's the significance of the coffee?'

'I'm so glad somebody has thought to ask me that question, before we finish. Well, it just goes to show that no matter how full your life –your jar – may seem, there's always room for a couple of cups of coffee with someone.' She then left the stage to rapturous applause.

Well, Kate, Jon, I hope you liked that story.

Notice that it's exactly what we have been doing at the end of each of our seven sessions with our coffee breaks. There's always time for a coffee with you. You've been patient on this journey of ours. I've enjoyed our sessions.

A couple of other pointers for you to consider and to make sense of everything, I hope.

Try and remember this to guide you through life:

*Watch your* **thoughts**, *they become your words*
*Watch your* **words**, *they become your actions*
*Watch your* **actions**, *they become your habits*
*Watch your* **habits**, *they become your character*
*Watch your* **character**, *it becomes your destiny.*

It's been said that we all walk backwards into the future and only see what a moment means when it's beyond our power to change it. As you discover that there has always been a better way to look at things that enhance your emotional well-being, don't blame yourself for mistakes you made in the past. My maxim is: 'Forgive yourself for not knowing what you didn't know before you learned it.'

Before I go, I wish you luck – and please accept this 'Royal Flush' to remind you of our time together and to help you lead a better life.

Thank you for listening.

## THE MIND IS *GIVEN* TO US, *WE* ARE NOT GIVEN TO THE MIND

## THINKING ISN'T SOMETHING THAT *HAPPENS* TO YOU, IT'S SOMETHING YOU *DO*

## FEELINGS AREN'T *FACTS*

## DON'T *BELIEVE* EVERYTHING YOU THINK

## THE WAY YOU *CHOOSE* TO SEE THE WORLD *CREATES* THE WORLD YOU SEE

# The discussion

'Well, folks. How did you get on with those transcripts?' said Jon as he came through the double doors and approached the table.

They all looked up at him excitedly. Jennifer was the first to speak. 'It's so inspiring, Jon! Maybe you should suggest to him that he turns it into a book. How about using the title from that first session – *Is That Your Card?*'

'Yes, I agree with you, Jennifer. Awesome. I felt as though I was there with you and Kate during your sessions, Jon,' said Courteney. 'Any chance of getting this guy Marc Sentus to come over to the UK?'

'Erm, there's a slight problem there,' Jon replied, 'I'll explain when Kate comes down.'

'What was that about the Royal Flush he gave you at the end of your last session, Jon?' asked Matthew.

'Oh, it was five cards with some real profound statements on them,' replied Jon.

'Can we see them? Courteney asked.

'How did I know I'd be asked about that?' said Jon, smiling. 'I know Jennifer will like these. I carry them in my wallet. Here, take a look and pass them around.'

Kate arrived, pulling her purse out of her handbag. 'Enjoyed reading?' she asked. They nodded. 'I'll get the coffee – *again!*'

'These statements on the cards, they're so – I don't know what the word is,' said Jennifer, having studied the cards intently.

'Life-affirming?' Tom offered.

'Yes – that's it, that will do,' Jennifer replied.

'Right, here's the coffee,' said Kate as she put the tray on the table in front of the long sofa. 'Trust you enjoyed the read?'

'We certainly did,' said the once-sceptical Matthew. 'I get this now. You know, most people just don't realise that you can actually watch your thinking. That you can be aware of the path that you're going down and question whether you're making sense of reality.'

'Don't chastise yourself, Matthew,' said Courteney. 'By the way, Kate, what was it that Jon was going to tell us about this chap Marc Sentus? He said to wait until you came down.'

Jon looked over to Kate and said, 'Do you want to tell them what happened, Kate?'

'OK,' she replied. 'Where do I start? The day after the final session, Jon and I went over to the building next door to see if we could talk to Marc and thank him with a gift. Trouble was, nobody had ever heard of him. Of course all we had was his voice on the recordings of the sessions. We took that over there later, in the hope that HR might recognise the voice, but when Jon played the audio – there was nothing there. *It was blank.*'

'What happened, then?' said Jennifer.

'Well, we asked around to see if anybody could recall seeing him, but no luck. And his name was not on the central head office books either.'

'That's so spooky,' said Jennifer.

'Yes,' Kate replied, 'because it was all OK the day before. That's when I did the transcripts.'

'And a good job you did too,' said Tom. 'Or we wouldn't have had this experience today.'

'Anyhow.' Jon leaned forward, his face becoming solemn. 'We spoke to one of the IT guys over there – a bright spark, I have to say. He looked at the name Marc Sentus. Then he pointed out something to Kate and me.

'He said if we take Marc as the short form of Marcus, as in Marcus Aurelius – then S-E-N as in the shortened form of Seneca

– then T-U-S as in the last letters of Epictetus – we get Marc Sentus.'

'Now that *is* spooky,' said Courteney, shivering a little in her seat. 'So what does that tell us?' she continued.

'It tells us that we just don't know,' replied Kate.

'So, Jon,' said Jennifer 'are you like . . . saying that he sort of didn't exist or something?'

Jon looked at Kate, hoping she would answer. 'We just don't know, Jennifer,' Kate said, 'nobody had ever seen him. All we have, luckily, is the transcript I made and the five playing cards.'

'We'll talk about this another time, shall we?' said Jon. 'We should head over to the station now, I think. We can't be late. I've still got some brushing up to do on my speech for this evening.'

They all got up. Kate headed over to pay for the coffee. 'You guys get the elevator, I'll just pay the bill quickly,' said Kate.

She caught up with them on the ground floor and they made their way towards the taxi rank. It started to rain. As she followed the others, Kate rummaged around for her umbrella. Her credit card, which she had still been holding, fell to the pavement.

'Excuse me. Is that your card?' Kate heard from behind her. The others carried on walking.

Kate looked up to see a hooded figure, its face hidden, handing her credit card to her. She took it. As she reached out, she saw the person was wearing a wristband inscribed with the words *'magic happens'*. Shocked, she called out to Jon but he was too far ahead. She looked round again for the hooded figure and there was nobody there. Nobody in sight.